WHITE INTO RED

A Study of the Assimilation of White Persons Captured by Indians

by

J. NORMAN HEARD

The Scarecrow Press, Inc.
Metuchen, N. J.   1973

Library of Congress Cataloging in Publication Data

Heard, Joseph Norman, 1922-
    White into red.

    Bibliography: p.
    1.   Indians of North America--Captivities.
2.   Assimilation (Sociology)   I.   Title.
E85.H38   301.24'1   72-13133
ISBN 0-8108-0581-2

To Steve, Diane and Bill

CONTENTS

PREFACE

In the small South Texas town of my boyhood half a century ago lived a dwindling number of citizens who knew the vanished frontier at first hand. Once in awhile some of them would gather at the old home place to talk of what J. Frank Dobie called "rocky times in Texas." My grandparents had been neighbors of the Thad Swift family and had discovered the massacre which Dobie described in his classic, A Vaquero of the Brush Country. Long before I was large enough to read the book I heard this story and many others while seated on my grandfather's lap wishing that I could have shared their adventures.

The story which fascinated me most was an account of the experiences of Grandma Strauch, still living in our town, who had been captured by Comanches in 1850. It was said that seventy-five years after her redemption you could still see the marks left on her legs by the rawhide thongs which the Indians had used to bind her to the back of a wild pony during their pell-mell retreat up the Nueces River. Perhaps it was this incident which sparked my life-long interest in Indian captivities.

Twenty years and a world war later it was my privilege to attend the University of Texas. Professor Dobie was gone, a casualty of a continuing skirmish with the Board of Regents, but Professors Walter Prescott Webb and H. Bailey Carroll were there to make the study of frontier history an unforgettable experience. Under their supervision I contributed articles to the Handbook of Texas and wrote a master's thesis on the Texas State Historical Association. While researching these topics I delved into the great collection of frontier narratives housed in the Eugene C. Barker History Center and the million-volume main library. My interest in racial relationships on the frontier was reinforced by frequent references to white captives who preferred the Indian life style to that of the cultural milieu from which they had been so abruptly removed.

Another twenty years passed and I was employed

vii

at the Louisiana State University Library at Baton Rouge. There I had the opportunity to work toward an advanced degree in American frontier history with a minor in anthropology. Permitted to choose a topic for investigation which straddled both fields, I grasped the opportunity to study assimilation of white children captured by Indians. This course work formed the core around which further investigations were made, leading to the formulation of conclusions based upon hundreds of case studies as to factors which facilitated or retarded the Indianization of white captives.

The original study was made under the supervision of Dr. William G. Haag, Alumni Professor of Anthropology, at L. S. U. I would like to express my sincere appreciation for his guidance and help. In addition, a great debt is owed to Dr. John L. Loos, Chairman of the Department of History, for his invaluable advice and assistance regarding the study of the American frontier, and to Dr. T. Harry Williams, Boyd Professor of History, for the inspiration of his lectures and for his enlightening criticism of my attempts at historical writing. Also I would like to acknowledge indebtedness to Mrs. Elsie Hebert Miller who typed the manuscript from very rough copy. And finally I express sincere appreciation to my wife, Mrs. Joyce Boudreaux Heard, for her patient understanding.

J. Norman Heard

ACKNOWLEDGMENTS

Grateful acknowledgment is made to the following for permission to use exerpts of copyrighted material:

The Historical Society of Western Pennsylvania for Mrs. Elvert M. Davis, "History of the Capture and Captivity of David Boyd from Cumberland County, Pennsylvania, 1756," in the Western Pennsylvania Historical Magazine, XIV (1931). Reprinted by permission.

Stackpole Books for C. Hale Sipe, Indian Wars of Pennsylvania. Copyright 1931. Reprinted by permission.

The University of Oklahoma Press for Thomas Wildcat Alford, Civilization, as Told to Florence Drake. Copyright 1936 by the University of Oklahoma Press. Carl Coke Rister, Border Captives. Copyright 1940 by the University of Oklahoma Press. Both reprinted by permission.

The University of Texas Press for Garcilaso de la Vega, The Florida of the Inca, translated and edited by John Grier Varner and Jeannette Johnson Varner. Copyright 1951 by the University of Texas Press. Reprinted by permission.

Yale University Press for The Papers of Benjamin Franklin, edited by Leonard W. Labaree, IV. Copyright 1961 by Yale University Press. Reprinted by permission.

The children of Geronimo's hostile Apache band, photographed in 1886. In foreground is a little white boy, Santiago McKinn, who was held captive by the Apaches for many months. At extreme left is a little Negro boy, also a captive when this band surrendered. (N. H. Rose Collection.)

Chapter 1

INTRODUCTION

This study analyzes narratives of captivity among the North American Indians in an attempt to ascertain why some prisoners preferred death to captivity, while others became so completely assimilated as to participate in raids against their relatives and former neighbors. An attempt is made to appraise the importance of such factors as the original cultural milieu, the age at time of capture, the duration of the captivity, and cultural characteristics of the captors, in determining the degree of assimilation. Some attention is given, also, to problems of readjustment by redeemed captives and to the assimilation of Indian children reared in white families.

Such a study was first suggested in 1926 by Dr. John R. Swanton, Smithsonian Institution ethnologist, in a perceptive but almost forgotten article. He pointed out that if there are psychological differences between races, evidence of this fact could be obtained by a study of individuals of one race who were captured at an early age by those of another and were brought up wholly immersed in the culture of the other. He believed that "if there is an actual psychological distinctness between the two, it should be recognized in the adopted or captured individuals as an element unaccountable on the basis of their cultural surroundings." Swanton sifted evidence obtained from a number of narratives of captivity and suggested that while they told much the same story the quantity of cases studied should be greatly increased and reciprocal cases investigated of primitive peoples held by whites.[1] Unfortunately, Swanton's article received little attention and his suggestions for further study have remained unfulfilled.[2]

The tradition of captive-taking goes back to prehistoric times among North American Indians. Centuries before white men came to these shores, captives were taken from neighboring tribes to replenish losses suffered in warfare or to obtain victims to torture in the spirit of revenge.

1

When warfare developed between Europeans and Indians,
white captives were taken for the same reasons and, in
addition, to hold for ransom or to gain favor with an allied
European government or colony. [3]

Indians in every region of the present United States
held at least a few white captives. But the majority were
taken in New England, northern New York, western Pennsylvania, western Virginia, Kentucky, the Great Plains, and
the Southwest. White men in the Southeast seemed, by and
large, to have avoided falling into the hands of the Indians.
In the northern Rockies and on the Pacific Coast, captive
taking was on a comparatively small scale.

Frontiersmen, with good reason, lived in constant
fear of Indian captivity. For men, capture frequently
ended in death by the most excruciating torments Indians
could learn from Europeans or devise for themselves. For
women, the fear was of lifelong bondage which frequently
included a fate which they considered worse than death.
Frontier people tried to keep always on guard against Indian
attack, but sometimes there was no way short of suicide
to avoid falling into the hands of raiders.

The Indians' favorite method of attack was to sur-
round a cabin during the pre-dawn hours and to rush the
family when the father came outdoors at first light. They
would massacre men, old women, and children too small
to travel, take the young women and older children captive,
and be well on their way back to their villages before neighbors could organize for pursuit. Frequently, the surviving
members of the family were compelled to carry the scalps
of their parents and little brothers and sisters, an experience which would seem likely to have instilled in them such
a hatred of Indians as to make assimilation impossible.

But there is an abundance of evidence that many captives quickly accepted the Indians as their own people and
came to regard the whites as enemies. Never was this
fact more clearly demonstrated than in November 1764 when
Colonel Henry Bouquet invaded the Shawnee stronghold on the
River Muskingum and compelled the Indians to release
hundreds of prisoners. A soldier named William Smith
wrote a graphic description of the scene:

> ... fathers and mothers recognizing and clasping
> their once-lost babes; husbands hanging round the

necks of their newly-recovered wives; sisters and
brothers unexpectedly meeting together after long
separation, scarce able to speak the same language, or, for some time, to be sure that they
were children of the same parents! In all these
interviews, joy and rapture inexpressible were seen,
while feelings of a very different nature were
painted in the looks of others; ... flying from place
to place in eager enquiries after relatives not
found!

The Indians, too, as if wholly forgetting their
usual savageness, bore a capital part in heightening
this most affecting scene. They delivered up
their beloved captives with the utmost reluctance;
shed torrents of tears over them, recommending
them to the care and protection of the commanding
officer. Their regard to them continued all the
time they remained in camp. They visited them
from day to day; and brought them what corn,
skins, horses, and other matters, they had bestowed on them, while in their families, accompanied with other presents, and all the marks of
the most sincere and tender affection. Nay, they
did not stop here, but, when the army marched,
some of the Indians solicited and obtained leave
to accompany their former captives all the way to
Fort Pitt, and employed themselves in hunting and
bringing provisions for them on the road. A young
Mingo carried this still further, and gave an instance of love which would make a figure even in
romance. A young woman of Virginia was among
the captives, to whom he had form'd so strong an
attachment, as to call her his wife. Against all
remonstrances of the imminent danger to which he
exposed himself by approaching to the frontier, he
persisted in following her....

Among the children who had been carried off young,
and had long lived with the Indians, it is not to
be expected that any marks of joy would appear on
being restored to their parents or relatives. Having
been accustomed to look upon the Indians as the
only connexions they had, having been tenderly
treated by them, and speaking their language, it
is no wonder that they considered their new state
in the light of a captivity, and parted from the
savages with tears.

But it must not be denied that there were even
some grown persons who shewed an unwillingness
to return. The Shawanese were obliged to bind
several of their prisoners and force them along
to the camp; and some women, who had been delivered up, afterwards found means to escape and
run back to the Indian towns. Some who could
not make their escape, clung to their savage acquaintance at parting, and continued many days in
bitter lamentations, even refusing sustenance. [4]

One reason for reluctance of some of the women to
leave their Indian husbands was the fact that they were
mothers of half-breed children. In some cases they were
accompanied by older children who were all white and
younger children who were half Indian. Many of them had
been with the Indians so long that they had forgotten their
native languages. When compiling a roll of captives it was
necessary to list them under such entries as "Cut-Arm" or
"German Girl" because they could no longer remember their
own names. By the time the roll was completed, two young
women named Rhoda Boyd and Elizabeth Studebaker had already escaped and fled into the wilderness to rejoin their
Indian families. The soldiers stood guard over others to
prevent them from running away. [5]

This scene, on a smaller scale, was repeated again
and again for the next one hundred and twenty years. While
in the vicinity of frontier forts throughout the West, white
persons painted their faces to conceal their identity from
officers who would have redeemed them. In Texas, whites
restored to their families after years of Comanche or Kiowa
captivity seized the first opportunity to escape to the red
men. The famous captive, Cynthia Ann Parker, who had
married a Comanche chief and bore him three children, was
prevented from rejoining the Indians. Unable to bridge the
chasm between civilizations and saddened by the death of
her youngest child, she grieved herself into an early grave. [6]
The trauma experienced by her aunt and fellow captive,
Rachel Plummer, was equally as shattering, but it occurred
as a result of inability to adjust to the Indian way of life.
She survived her captivity by only a few months and concluded
her narrative with prophetic words: "With these remarks I
submit the following pages ... feeling assured that before
they are published, the hand that penned them will be cold
in death. "[7]

It is probable that the majority of captives did not remain in Indian hands long enough for the assimilation process
to make substantial headway.   Many were killed during the
journey to the Indian villages or were tortured upon arrival.
Others were ransomed quickly by relatives or traders.   Some
were sold to an allied European nation within a few months.
A surprisingly large number escaped, sometimes killing their
captors in the process.   But the fact remains that hundreds
of white captives became almost completely Indianized.   Many
of them eventually returned to their white families, and by
analyzing their own statements, as well as those of witnesses
who described their attempts to readjust to white civilization,
some light may be thrown on racial assimilation.

Because this study is based primarily on evidence
presented in narratives of captivity, the question of the authenticity and credibility of sources must be considered.
While scholars have demonstrated confidence in many of these
narratives by citing them in their bibliographies, little by
way of evaluation has been published.   Caution in the use of
such sources was advised by Dwight L. Smith, who appraised
Shawnee captivity ethnography with the intent of determining
the value of narratives of captivity to ethnologists and historians.   He called attention to the need to consider the ob-
jectives of the former captive in writing of his experiences:
"Some of their accounts manifestly were written to arouse
sentiment against the Indians, others to warn those who en-
tertained ideas of travel and settlement in the Indian country,
and still others for public consumption as adventure stories."

> The results of this study show that the captivity
> can be considered as only a fragmentary source of
> ethnohistory for the Old Northwest.   The captivity
> narrative ... is one of the most readable types of
> American literature ever produced.   As a part of
> this story the habits, customs, and ways of life of
> the Indian garnish the simple details of the account.
> These things are of interest to the ethnologist and
> historian.   In an objective appraisal, nevertheless,
> these items cannot all be accepted at face value.
> The circumstances under which they were originally
> observed and the reasons for which they were
> written must be considered before they can be used
> totally or in part by ethnologists and historians.

Smith conceded, however, that studies of captivities are
legitimate scholarly pursuits, as the basis for the narratives

was a common experience of hundreds of pioneers. [8]

R. W. G. Vail, historian-bibliographer, made a major
contribution to scholarship with his comprehensive biblio-
graphical essay, The Voice of the Old Frontier, by appraising the authenticity of narratives of captivity. He acknowledged that the captive, like most frontiersmen, was prone to
exaggerate--"to draw the long bow"--but he emphasized that
narratives of captivity are "simple, vivid, direct and, generally, accurate pictures of the exciting and often harrowing
adventures of their authors" which are "of importance to the
historian and biographer, the ethnologist, the sociologist, the
natural scientist, and the medical historian. "[9]

The Kentucky historian, Willard Rouse Jillson, has
made extensive use of narratives of captivity. Noting that
frontier literature is enhanced by hundreds of accounts of
captivities, he stated that "many of these narratives, told by
returning white captives, are not only dependable, but are
truthful and informative as to the life, practice, and philoso-
phies of the American Indian. "[10]

Among leading historians who have written scholarly
introductions to reprints of narratives of captivity are Walter
Prescott Webb, Charles M. Andrews, and Milo M. Quaife.
Webb's edition of Nelson Lee's captivity contains some of the
most amazing adventures of any narrative of its kind, including the assertion that Lee's life was spared because he owned
an alarm watch which fascinated the Indians.   The Comanches
almost never spared the life of an adult male captive, but
Webb regarded the story as authentic.   "It is his account of
life among the Indians that makes this book of unique value,"
Webb wrote.   "The story he tells is absorbing, but the information he conveys about how the Comanches lived before
they were affected by the white man is invaluable. "[11]

Aside from Swanton, few ethnologists in the United
States have voiced opinions on the usefulness of the captivity
narrative.   A distinguished Canadian scholar, Marius Barbeau, has devoted more attention to the subject than have his
colleagues below the international boundary.   He believes
they "constitute a valuable source of information still un-
tapped. " In appraising the ethnological materials in the
magnificent Greenwood Collection of captive narratives he
asserted that "their value is enhanced by the candor of the
observers who found themselves among the natives before the
ancient customs had been abandoned, and the enthnographers

had entered the field. "[12]

Because the taking of captives by North American Indians was halted in the 1880's it is no longer possible for an
ethnologist to gain first-hand knowledge of assimilation
through interviews.   But in South America this is not the
case, for white captives yet may be roaming the jungles of
the Rio Negro and Orinoco Basins.   A remarkable study of
captivity and assimilation was published recently by an Italian
anthropologist, Ettore Biocca, based upon interviews with
Helen Valero, who had escaped after twenty years of captivity
in that region.   "The opportunity of studying an unknown and
wild group of Indians through the testimony of a woman
prisoner who succeeded in returning to the world of the white
man, is a fortunate and exceptional event which, it seems,
has no parallel in the history of American ethnology, " Biocca
asserted.

The similarity of Helen Valero's experiences to those
of North American female captives is striking.   In her grip-
ping narrative she tells of captivity at the age of twelve after
having been shot in the stomach with a poisoned arrow, of
being beaten for trying to escape, of learning the languages
of a number of tribes (for she was captured and recaptured
several times during intertribal warfare), of becoming reconciled to the Indian way of life, of her marriage and mother-
hood, of the murder of her husband, and of her abduction by
a cruel master which resulted in rekindling the desire to
escape.   After her return to civilization she even experienced
the same rejection by relatives which had befallen some
North American captives who had married Indians.   The experiences which Helen Valero described are in every regard
as amazing as any which have been recorded in North
American narratives of captivity, yet Biocca expressed full
confidence in her story, having interviewed many individuals
in the jungle who confirmed the incidents she described. [13]

A majority of the case studies included in this mono-
graph have been listed in standard bibliographies or cited by
historians or ethnologists.   It is believed, therefore, that
while individual narratives may contain inaccuracies and ex-
aggerations, taken in the aggregate they provide a generally
reliable source of information on assimilation.

Notes

1. John R. Swanton, "Notes on the Mental Assimilation of
    Races," in Journal of the Washington Academy of
    Sciences, XVI (1926), 493, 502.

2. William N. Fenton, American Indian and White Relations
    to 1830. (Chapel Hill, 1957), 18.

3. Frederick Webb Hodge, Handbook of Indians North of
    Mexico. (Washington, 1912), I, 203-6.

4. William Smith, An Historical Account of the Expedition
    Against the Ohio Indians in the Year 1764. (Phila-
    delphia, 1765), 26-27, 29.

5. Dale Van Every, Forth to the Wilderness. (New York,
    1961), 217-18.

6. The Handbook of Texas. (Austin, 1952), II, 335.

7. Carl Coke Rister, Border Captives. (Norman, 1940),
    68-76.

8. Dwight L. Smith, "Shawnee Captivity Ethnography," in
    Ethnohistory, II (1955), 29-31, 37.

9. R. W. G. Vail, The Voice of the Old Frontier. (New
    York, 1949), 27.

10. Willard Rouse Jillson, Indian Captivities of the Early
     West. (Louisville, 1953), 15.

11. Walter Prescott Webb, introduction to Nelson Lee,
     Three Years Among the Comanches. (Norman, 1957),
     ix-x.

12. Marius Barbeau, "Indian Captivities," in American
     Philosophical Society Proceedings, XCIV (1950), 531.

13. Ettore Biocca, Yanoama. (New York, 1970), 1-13.

Chapter 2

A CONTEST OF CIVILIZATIONS

In every initial contact between North American Indians and Europeans the natives were hospitable and helpful. But the whites, hungry for land, trade goods, and free labor, soon antagonized many of the tribes. A type of warfare evolved which was strongly racial, so much so that whites returning from an unsuccessful attempt to overtake marauding warriors would fall upon the first unoffending Indians they met. The Indians countered white incursions with equal ferocity. [1] In the course of this conflict, which lasted four centuries and spanned the continent, captive taking was an important element.

While the Indian was a formidable raider, over the long pull he was no match for the better armed frontiersmen who swarmed into his country or the better disciplined troops frequently called upon to punish the tribes for striking back at treaty violators. It is clear in retrospect that the end result was inevitable. Wilcomb E. Washburn, Smithsonian Institution ethnologist, analyzed the situation succinctly: "The two societies could not, or would not, reconcile themselves to each other. The individualism of the European, for example, would not accommodate itself to the communal character of the original American, nor could the communal Indian society accommodate itself to European individualism. The two human elements fought for the same land base, and the loser might retain his physical existence but almost invariably he lost the culture and the land that gave his life meaning. "[2]

Benjamin Franklin was among the few men of his time who understood the Indian-white relationship as a contest of civilizations in which the red man, no less than the white, was convinced of the superiority of his own way of life. In a letter to a friend, Franklin commented that the

> proneness of human nature to a life of ease, of
> freedom, from care and labour appears strongly

9

in the little success that has hitherto attended every
attempt to civilize our American Indians, in their
present way of living, almost all their Wants are
supplied by the spontaneous Productions of Nature,
with the addition of very little labour, if hunting
and fishing may indeed be called labour when Game
is so plenty, they visit us frequently, and see the
advantages that Arts, Sciences, and compact Society
procure us, they are not deficient in natural understanding and yet they have never shown any Inclination to change their manner of life for ours, or to
learn any of our Arts; When an Indian Child has
been brought up among us, taught our language and
habituated to our Customs, yet if he goes to see
his relations and make one Indian Ramble with them,
there is no persuading him ever to return, and that
this is not natural merely as Indians, but as men,
is plain from this, that when white persons of
either sex have been taken prisoner young by the
Indians, and lived awhile among them, tho' ransomed by their Friends, and treated with all imaginable tenderness to prevail with them to stay
among the English, yet in a Short time they became
disgusted with our manner of life, and the care and
pains that are necessary to support it, and take the
first opportunity of escaping again into the Woods,
from whence there is no reclaiming them.   One
instance I remember to have heard, where the person was to be brought home to possess a good
Estate; but finding some care necessary to keep it
together, he relinquished it to a younger Brother,
reserving to himself nothing but a gun and a match-
Coat, with which he took his way again to the
Wilderness.

Franklin then recounted an incident which illustrates
the Indians' belief in their own innate superiority:

The little value Indians set on what we prize so
highly under the name of Learning appears from a
pleasant passage that happened some years since at
a Treaty between one of our Colonies and the Six
Nations; when everything had been settled to the
Satisfaction of both sides, and nothing remained but
a mutual exchange of civilities, the English Commissioners told the Indians, they had in their
Country a College for the instruction of Youth who

were taught various languages, Arts, and Sciences;
that there was a particular foundation in favour of
the Indians to defray the expense of the Education
of any of their sons who should desire to take the
Benefit of it. And now if the Indians would accept
of the Offer, the English would take a dozen of
their brightest lads and bring them up in the Best
manner; The Indians after consulting on the proposal replied that it was remembered some of their
Youths had been formerly educated in that College,
but it had been observed that for a long time after
they returned to their Friends, they were absolutely
good for nothing being neither acquainted with the
true methods of killing deer, catching Beaver or
surprizing an enemy. The Proposition however,
they looked on as a mark of kindness and good will
of the English to the Indian Nations which merited
a grateful return; and therefore if the English
Gentlemen would send a dozen or two of their
Children to Onondago the great Council would take
care of their Education, bring them up in really
what was the best manner and make men of them.[3]

Few redeemed white captives have extolled the superiority of the Indian life style (although many voluntarily returned to it.) But such a claim has been made by a talented
writer who chose to live his life as an Indian.   James Willard
Schultz, an eighteen-year-old member of a prominent New
York family, was preparing to enter West Point in 1877 when
he went to Montana for a summer's buffalo hunting.   He developed an affection for the wild, free life, married a Blackfoot maiden, and remained with the Indians until after they
were driven onto the reservation.   "Alas! Alas!" he wrote,

why could not this simple life have continued? Why
must the railroads and the swarms of settlers have
invaded that wonderful land, and robbed its lords
of all that made life worth living? They knew not
care, nor hunger, nor want of any kind. From my
window here I hear the roar of the great city, and
see the crowds hurrying by ... 'bound to the wheel, '
and there is no escape from it except by death.
And this is civilization! I, for one, maintain that
there is no satisfaction, no happiness in it. The
Indians of the plains back in those days of which I
write, alone knew what was perfect content and
happiness, and that, we are told, is the chief end

and aim of men--to be free from want, and worry,
and care.   Civilization will never furnish it,   except
to the very,   very few. [4]

In many respects the experiences of Charles A. Eastman paralleled those of Schultz, but in reverse.   Eastman,
a Sioux Indian, was raised by an uncle (a great warrior) with
the principal motive of avenging the death of his father, believed to have been killed by the whites.   But when the boy
was fifteen his father suddenly walked into camp, related
that he had accepted the white way of life, and persuaded the
young warrior to get an education.   Charles eventually married a white woman and became a doctor and a writer but,
like Schultz, he saw much in the Indian life style which was
lacking in white civilization:

> ... when nature is at her best, and provides
> abundantly for the savage, it seems to me that no
> life is happier than his! Food is free--lodging
> free--everything free! All were alike rich in the
> summer, and again, all were alike poor in the
> winter....   The Indian boy enjoyed such a life as
> almost all boys dream of and would choose for
> themselves if they were permitted to do so. [5]

Eastman clearly perceived that the Indian could not
compete in a world controlled by white men's advanced tech-
nology.   He dedicated himself to leading his people to accept
civilization.   But after many disillusioning experiences with
corrupt government officials and business leaders he found
little to praise in their way of life.   "Why, " he asked, "do
we find so much evil and wickedness practiced by the nations
composed of professedly 'Christian' individuals?"

> The pages of history are full of licensed murder
> and the plundering of weaker and less developed
> peoples, and obviously the world to-day has not
> outgrown this system.   Behind the material and
> intellectual splendor of ... civilization, primitive
> savagery and cruelty and lust hold sway, undi-
> minished, and as it seems, unheeded.   When I let
> go of my simple, instinctive nature religion, I
> hoped to gain something far loftier as well as more
> satisfying to the reason.   Alas! It is also more
> confusing and contradictory.   The higher and
> spiritual life, though first in theory, is clearly
> secondary, if not entirely neglected, in actual prac-

> tice.   When I reduce civilization to its lowest
> terms, it becomes a system of life based upon
> trade.   The dollar is the measure of value, and
> might still spells right....[6]

Has this contest between civilizations relevance to a
study of assimilation of captives?   Yes, in the sense that it
suggests a primary reason why individuals of both races who
experienced both civilizations so frequently preferred the Indian life style.   It would appear that Indian family life offered
much to the fulfillment of the individual which was lacking in
the more advanced civilization.   Charles A. Eastman believed
that Indians' "love for one another is stronger than that of
any civilized people."[7]   Thomas Wildcat Alford, a Shawnee
who attended boarding school, asserted that "Indian parents
felt their responsibility keenly and paid more attention to
training their children than does the civilized white family."[8]

And the evidence presented in narratives of captivity
strongly suggests that Indians loved their adopted white
children with an instinctive openness which would be difficult
for white parents to exceed.   Nowhere, perhaps, is this fact
better illustrated than in the account given by Thomas Wildcat Alford of the experience of his great grandmother, a
white captive of the Shawnees:

> The scouts brought the baby to the chief's wife,
> who was childless.   She loved the little white girl
> very dearly, and cared for her as tenderly as she
> knew how to do.   The child grew and played hap-
> pily with the Indian children.

When the girl was fourteen she was given up, along
with numerous other captives, under terms of a treaty.   "But
she loved the Indians and their wild, free way of living, and
pined for her foster mother so much that she was very unhappy when separated from her."   She seized the first opportunity to escape and made her way across a trackless wilderness to rejoin the tribe.

> In the meantime the girl's foster mother, the wife
> of the Indian chief, had grieved so deeply over the
> loss of her daughter that it was thought she would
> not live.   She refused to eat food, and pined away.
> Finally she was no longer able to go about, but lay
> on her bed in an exhausted condition, seemingly
> waiting for her life to leave her body....

Then, suddenly, "the young girl approached, and they were clasped in each other's arms.... The foster mother was no longer ill; she rapidly regained her strength, and lived to an old age." The girl eventually married an Indian and bore him eight children. [9]

Here, then, is one factor facilitating the assimilation of white captives. Taken at an impressionable age, cherished by Indian adopted parents, introduced to a life of freedom and adventure, it is understandable that many of them lost the desire to return to the grinding toil of a white family on the frontier.

Notes

1. John Collier, The Indians of the Americas. (New York, 1947), 190-98.

2. The Indian and the White Man. (New York, 1964), xii.

3. Benjamin Franklin letter to Peter Collinson, May 9, 1753, The Papers of Benjamin Franklin. (New Haven, 1961), 481-83.

4. J. W. Schultz, My Life as an Indian. (Boston and New York, 1935), 46.

5. Charles A. Eastman, Indian Boyhood. (Boston, 1937), 16-18.

6. Charles A. Eastman, From the Deep Woods to Civilization. (Boston, 1916), 194.

7. Ibid., 6.

8. From Civilization, as Told to Florence Drake, by Thomas Wildcat Alford, pp. 18-21. Copyright 1936 by the University of Oklahoma Press.

9. Ibid., 1-3.

Chapter 3

FAMILY BACKGROUND AND
RESISTANCE TO ASSIMILATION

The theory has been advanced by more than one
scholar that preexisting conditions determined whether a white
captive readily adopted or strongly resisted the Indian way of
life.   Such characteristics as innate racial or familial superiority, high or low intelligence, gentle or rough upbringing,
and good or poor religious training, have been suggested as
determinants of the rate and degree of assimilation.   This
chapter and the next seek to determine whether a significant
correlation is indicated between the captive's original cultural
milieu and the extent of his adoption of the Indian way of life.

Early in this century a relative of Frances Slocum
(the famous "lost sister of Wyoming") presented an interesting if highly debatable paper advocating heredity as the determining factor in assimilation.   In an address to the Anthropology Section of the American Association for the Advancement of Science, Charles E. Slocum (M. D. , LL. B. ,
Ph. D.) theorized that although Frances was captured at the
age of five and forgot her native language and even her given
name during sixty years of life with the Indians, her Quaker
inheritance enabled her to resist the savage practices of her
captors and to influence the Indians to improve their way of
life.

He asserted that Frances Slocum's captivity was unique
in the regard that her ancestors were not typical "rough and
ready" frontier people.   She was a "delicate, timid, female
child rudely transferred from a quiet family in the Society of
Friends to a savage environment among hideous strangers in
time of war."[1]   The scenes which she witnessed at the time
she was captured "were so savage and shocking as to soon
obscure all memory of details of her environment and a brief
period of parental training ... and to leave her as a foundation for a worthy future character only the influence of
heredity. "   This heritage enabled her to resist the more
savage traits of Indian character while thoroughly acquiring

15

their milder habits.   "The kindly disposition of her Quaker
ancestors, the good-will-to-all-persons, the for-generations-
inbred considerate mood governing expressions and actions,
curbing and disciplining impulse to the enthronement of rea-
son--all had left an indelible impress on her psychic life. "[2]

   It would seem that if the facts bear out Slocum's
theory, a beginning has been made toward answering the
question posed by Swanton as to whether an actual psychological distinctness exists between races.   If Frances had
completely forgotten her earlier environment and yet resisted
adoption of traits which were common to females among her
captors,   some indication of such psychological differences
between races would be discernible.   Such evidence as is
available indicates, however, that she retained remarkably
vivid recollections of her life before captivity, describing the
house in which the family lived before moving to the Wyoming Valley and even the great heap of money counted out on
the table which her father received when selling the place. [3]

   While no evidence was found to support the theory that
cultural differences between Frances and her Indian companions were due to heredity, there is some indication that at
least minor differences did exist.   After settling on a reservation she became wealthy by Indian standards, lived in a
comfortable home and kept it spotlessly clean.   She ate on
dishes which she washed immediately after the meal.   When
visitors remarked on the practice, she credited her white
mother with having trained her in habits of cleanliness. [4]   It
would appear, then, that her early parental training, brief
as it was, may have been instrumental in the retention of
certain characteristics which differed from those of her
adopted people.

   Did these characteristics enable her to influence the
Indians to improve their way of life?   There is little evidence to support the claim.   She was respected as an influ-
ential woman by her neighbors, but this might be expected
of a wealthy widow of a chief.   Her husband, so far as is
known, did not follow the warpath, but this fact is explained
by his deafness rather than her salutary influence.   Violence
was not unknown in her immediate Indian family, for one
son-in-law was killed in a drunken brawl and her grand-
daughter was poisoned by a rejected suitor. [5]

   Dr. Slocum's belief that his relative's captivity was
unique is not supported by the facts.   By no means did all

other captives come from environments in which refinement
was lacking. His theory, however, that a captive reared in
sheltered surroundings would react differently from those of
"common" frontier stock when thrown into a primitive environment merits investigation. The three case studies which
follow are of female captives who fall into this category.

Captivity of Frances Slocum

Frances Slocum was captured in the Wyoming Valley
of Pennsylvania on November 2, 1778. She was five years
old at the time and she remained with the Indians sixty-eight
years. Her mother and brothers made many fruitless trips
into the wilderness trying to find her and offering large re-
wards for her return. Many years passed before the search
was abandoned. Then, in 1837, a white man who could speak
the language of the Miami tribe chanced to visit an Indian
home near the Wabash River and discovered that the head of
the family was a white woman. She told him that her name
was Slocum and that she had never revealed her identity because she was afraid her relatives would compel her to leave
her Indian family. Now that she was old she was willing for
her white relatives, if any still lived, to learn of her where-
abouts.

As a result of this meeting, Frances Slocum's
brothers visited her and urged her to return with them to
Pennsylvania, if not to stay, at least for a visit. But she
declined:

> I can not. I can not. I am an old tree. I can
> not move about. I was a sapling when they took
> me away. It is all gone past. I am afraid I
> should die and never come back. I am happy here.
> I shall die here and lie in that grave-yard, and
> they will raise the pole at my grave with the white
> flag on it, and the Great Spirit will know where to
> find me. I should not be happy with my white
> relatives. I am glad enough to see them, but I
> can not go. I can not go. I have done. [6]

Frances gave a brief account of her captivity to her
brother, Joseph. Statements which throw some light on the
course of assimilation follow:

> Three Delaware Indians came suddenly to our house.

They killed and scalped a man near the door.   A
boy ran into the house, and I hid under the stair-
case.   The Indians came into the house and went
up stairs....   They carried us through the bushes.
I looked back, but saw no one except my mother.
They carried us over the mountains--it seemed to
me a long way--to a cave....   I was very tired,
and I lay down on the ground, and cried until I fell
asleep.

The next morning we set off early, and we traveled
many days in the woods....   They ... were very
kind to me; when they had any thing to eat, I always had the best; when I was tired, they carried
me in their arms; and in a short time I began to
feel better, and stopped crying. [7]

Finally they reached the Delaware village of Chief
Tack-horse, which was to become her first Indian home.

Early one morning Tack-horse took me and dressed
my hair in the Indian fashion, and painted my face.
He then dressed me up, and put on me beautiful
wampum, and made me look very fine.   I was much
pleased with the wampum.

... I was now adopted by Tack-horse and his wife
in the place of one they had lost a short time before, and they gave me her name.   When the Indians lose a child, they often adopt some one in its
place, and treat that one in all respects as their
own.   This is the reason why they so often carry
off the children of white people. [8]

By the time she was thirteen, Frances had come to
regard the Indians as her people and to fear the possibility of
being recaptured by the whites.   Upon reaching puberty it
seemed only natural for her to marry an Indian.

I was always treated kindly by the Delawares; and
while I lived with them I was married to a Delaware by the name of Little Turtle.   He afterward
left me and went west of the Mississippi.   I would
not go with him.   My old mother staid here, and I
chose to stay with her.   My adopted father could
talk English, and so could I while he lived.   It has
now been a long time since I forgot it all.

> The Delawares and Miamis were then living to-
> gether as one people. I was afterward married to
> a Miami, a chief.... We came to this reserve
> about twenty-four years ago. I had no children by
> my first husband, but by the last one I had four.... [9]

A few years after Frances was found by her relatives,
the United States Government moved the Miamis west of the
Mississippi. Joseph Slocum successfully petitioned Congress
to grant his sister permission to remain on her land. But
Frances was never content after the Indians were removed.
She was constantly concerned that her new white neighbors
coveted the square mile which Congress had given her. Although her widowed daughter remained with her, all of her
friends had departed and she was surrounded by a way of life
which was utterly foreign to her.

> Despairing of the return of the scenes of the past,
> she sighed for release from the associations and
> vices of civilization. Contrasting the freedom and
> romance of savage life with the thirst of gain and
> the overreaching policy of a white frontier settle-
> ment, she thought she had truly fallen upon evil
> times, and was really weary of life.... During
> her last sickness ... Francis Slocum refused all
> medical aid, declaring that as her people were
> gone, and she was surrounded by strangers, she
> wished to live no longer. She departed this life
> March 9, 1847. [10]

Captivity of Eunice Williams

Eunice Williams was taken by Iroquois Indians during
a raid on Deerfield, Massachusetts, in 1704. She was seven
years old at the time. Her mother was killed during the
raid and her father, brothers and sisters were captured. Her
father, John Williams, was a Puritan minister and Eunice
had been reared under the strictest principles of that faith.
Carried to Canada and converted to Catholicism, she became
so completely assimilated that in three years' time she refused the opportunity to return home.

Like Frances Slocum, Eunice was treated kindly on
her journey to the Indian village. Her father noted that she
was carried all the way and looked after with a great deal
of tenderness.

A summation of correspondence and other records
relative to many attempts to reclaim the child was made by
Emma Lewis Coleman in her valuable study of New England
captives carried to Canada:

> She was taken to the Sault Saint-Louis.   The Jesuit
> at the Mission would not allow her father to go
> there because the Maquas 'would as soon part with
> their hearts as the child, ' but Governor de Vaud-
> reuil, angry and insistent, went 'in his own per-
> son' to the fort with Mr. Williams and the child
> was brought into her father's presence.   She re-
> peated to him her Catechism, for she had already
> learned to read, he says, and she complained that
> the Indians 'profaned God's Sabbath' and that she
> was forced 'to say some prayers in Latin, ' but she
> did not 'understand one word of them' and hoped it
> did her no harm.

> 'The Governor labored much for her redemption; at
> last he had the promise of it, in case he would
> procure for them an Indian girl in her stead. '
> When, however, the Indian girl was offered she
> was refused.   So was 'An hundred pieces of eight.'

> 'His lady went over, to have begged her from them,
> but all in vain; she is there still and has forgotten
> to speak English. ' So wrote her father immediately
> after his own return to Boston.

Many attempts were made to persuade Eunice to return to her people but she resolutely refused.   Prisoners
held in New England were offered in exchange for her and
the proposition was accepted by the French, but to no avail.
The daughter of a steadfast Protestant minister had become
converted to Catholicism and learned to love her Indian masters.

> In 1713 John Schuyler, youngest brother of Colonel
> Peter, was sent to Montreal, but in spite of his
> 'indefatigueable Pains' he could not bring back
> Eunice.   Eunice had already been baptized and
> married to a young Indian.   The priest told Schuy-
> ler that he had been unwilling to marry them, even
> going away from the fort, but the two young people
> protested that with or without the service they would
> live together and he had married them 'after some
> days past. '

> Eunice went to the priest's house to see Schuyler,
> 'with the Indian She was Married to, both together.
> She looking very poor in body, bashful in the face,
> but proved harder than Steel in her breast. '

> During 'allmost two hours time' that Schuyler, the
> priest and 'Indian Languester' talked to her; using
> 'fair offers' of going to Deerfield and returning;
> and 'long Solicitations' only two words--'Jaghte
> oghte' did she utter.   'May be not, ' which 'amongst
> the Indians is a plaine denyall. '   Then, 'being very
> Sorrowful' Schuyler 'took her by the hand and left
> her. '

In 1714 Rev. John Williams returned to Montreal to
make a final attempt to obtain his daughter.   His account of
the visit provides an interesting insight into the assimilation
of Eunice Williams and other young girls who were taken
captive during the attack on Deerfield.

> And she is yet obstinately resolved to live and dye
> here, and will not so much as give me one plea-
> sant look.   It's beyond my ability, in the contents
> of a letter, to make you understand how ours here
> are besotted.   We are like to be very unsuccess-
> ful.   We take all the best methods we can, and
> put on all the patience we have; but the English are
> so naturalized to the customs and manners of the
> French and Indians and have forgotten the English
> tongue, and are so many of them married or gotten
> into nunneries ... that I think it would be far
> easier to gain twice the number of French and In-
> dians to go with us than English. [12]

Captivity of Mary Boyeau

Fanny Kelly, a young married woman, was captured
by Sioux Indians in 1864.   During her captivity she encountered another young white woman and included an account of
their conversation in her own narrative of captivity:

> I was so reduced in strength and spirit, that noth-
> ing but the dread of the scalping-knife urged my
> feet from task to task; and now, returning toward
> the tipi, with my heavy bucket, I was startled to
> behold a fair-faced beautiful young girl sitting

there, dejected and worn, like myself, but bearing
the marks of loveliness and refinement, despite her
neglected covering.

Almost doubting my reason, for I had become unsettled in my self-reliance, and even sanity, I
feared to address her, but stood spell-bound, gaz-
ing in her sad brown eyes and drooping, pallid
face.

The chief stood near the entrance of the tipi ...
watching the interview with amusement.   He
offered me a book, which chanced to be one of the
Willson's readers, stolen from our wagons, and
bade me show it to the stranger.

I approached the girl, who instantly held out her
hand, and said: 'What book is that?'[13]

Mary Boyeau then told her story:

'My name is Mary Boyeau; these people call me
Madee.   I have been among them since the massacre in Minnesota, and am now in my sixteenth
year.   My parents were of French descent, but we
lived in the State of New York, until my father, in
pursuit of his peculiar passion for the life of a
naturalist and a man of science, sold our eastern
home, and came to live on the shores of Spirit
Lake, Minnesota.

'The Indians had watched about our place, and regarded what they had seen of my father's chemical
apparatus with awe and fear.   Perhaps they suspected him of working evil charms in his labora-
tory....

'I can not tell; I only know that we were among the
first victims of the massacre, and that all of my
family were murdered except myself, and, I fear,
one younger sister.'

'You fear!' said I.   'Do you not hope that she escaped?'

The poor girl shook her head, 'From a life like
mine death is an escape,' she said, bitterly.

'Oh! it is fearful! and a sin to rush unbidden into God's presence, but I can not live through another frightful winter.

'No, I must and will die if no relief comes to me. For a year these people regarded me as a child, and then a young man of their tribe gave a horse for me, and carried me to his tipi as his wife. '

'Do you love your husband?' I asked.

'Love a savage, who bought me to be a drudge and slave!' she repeated.   'No! I hate him as I hate all that belong to this fearful bondage.   He has another wife and child.   Thank God!' she added, with a shudder, 'that I am not a mother!'

Misery and the consciousness of her own degraded life seemed to have made this poor young creature desperate; and, looking at her toil-worn hands and scarred arms, I saw the signs of abuse and cruelty; her feet, too, were bare, and fearfully bruised and travel-marked.

'Does he ill treat you?'   I inquired.

'His wife does, ' she answered.   'I am forced to do all manner of slavish work, and when my strength fails, I am urged on by blows.   Oh!   I do so fearfully dread the chilling winters, without proper food or clothing; and I long to lie down and die, if God's mercy will only permit me to escape from this hopeless imprisonment.   I have nothing to expect now.   I did once look forward to release, but that is all gone. '

... she had never attempted to escape, nor did she seem to think it possible to get away from her present life, so deep was the despair into which long-continued suffering had plunged her. [14]

While these three captivities were spaced over a century and a half and took place in different regions, there are a number of similarities which make them useful for comparative studies of assimilation.   All three captives came from homes in which education and religious training were emphasized.   All three witnessed the killing of members of

their families by the Indians.   All three were treated at first
by their captors as children.   All three eventually married
Indians.

    Yet Eunice Williams and Frances Slocum lived con-
tentedly to extreme old age with their captors, while Mary
Boyeau courted death as an escape from the Indian way of
life.   These cases and others too numerous for inclusion
would appear to indicate that factors other than superior
familial characteristics, refined upbringing, or religious
training, acted as determinants in the process of assimilation.

Notes

1.   Charles Elihu Slocum, History of Frances Slocum. (De-
       fiance, Ohio, 1908), unpaged preface.

2.   Ibid. , 36-37.

3.   George Peck, Wyoming.   (New York, 1858), 270-74.

4.   Ibid. , 267-68.

5.   Ibid. , 270-74.

6.   Ibid. , 262.

7.   Ibid. , 274-75.

8.   Ibid. , 276.

9.   Ibid. , 279.

10. Ibid. , 282-83.

11. Swanton, "Notes on the Mental Assimilation of Races, "
       493.

12. Emma Lewis Coleman, New England Captives Carried to
       Canada. (Portland, Me. , 1925), II, 44-58.

13. Fanny Kelly, Narrative of My Captivity Among the Sioux
       Indians. (Hartford, 1872), 112-13.

14. Ibid. , 114-16.

Chapter 4

NATIONAL ORIGINS AND INDIANIZATION

Still to be considered within the general context of the
original milieu as determinant in assimilation is the theory
that racial or national origins influenced the degree of Indianization. Carl Coke Rister, a frontier historian who has
written extensively about Indian warfare in the Southwest,
asserted that it "was easier for a Wichita woman to adapt
herself to the lodge of a Comanche warrior than it was for
a Mexican mestizo woman or peon to do so; and such a
change for an Anglo-American housewife could hardly be
made without social and spiritual metamorphoses.

" ... the average Mexican ... lived in a jacal hut of
pole-mud construction with dirt floor, and subsisted on mis-
erably poor fare. He must take no great cultural step,
therefore, in going from the life he had lived to that required by his captors. ... records prove that 'Indianized'
Mexican women were found more frequently in Apache, Comanche, and Kiowa camps than were Anglo-Americans. "[1]

Original sources do indicate that Mexican captives
frequently became completely assimilated. Thomas Fitzpatrick, veteran scout and Kiowa Indian agent, reported that
the Mexican males adopted into the tribe became skillful
marauders while females frequently were selected as wives.[2]
But is there evidence that captives of other ethnic origins
were more successful in resisting assimilation? A majority
of captives were taken from three stocks--Anglo-American,
German-American, or Mexican. In order to sift evidence of
assimilation, the experiences of six captives, three males
and three females, will be presented as written or related
by themselves.

Captivity of Mary Jemison

Mary Jemison was born on shipboard about 1743. She
was the daughter of Scotch-Irish immigrants, that hardy

25

breed of land-seekers who left an indelible mark on the
American frontier.   The family settled in the Pennsylvania
wilderness.   In 1758 the French and Indian War brought devastation to their doorstep.   Mary was captured by marauding Shawnees and lived the remainder of her life (75 years)
as an Indian maiden and squaw.   Shortly before her death,
she told her life story to Dr. James E. Seaver.   Included
were the following incidents which are of interest in analyzing the process of Indianization:

> In the afternoon we came in sight of Fort Pitt (as
> it is now called), where we were halted while the
> Indians performed some customs upon their pris-
> oners which they deemed necessary. ... the In-
> dians combed the hair of the young man, the boy
> and myself, and then painted our faces and hair
> red, in the finest Indian style.   We were then con-
> ducted into the fort, where we received a little
> bread, and were then shut up and left to tarry alone
> through the night.   ... it was not long before I was
> in some measure relieved by the appearance of two
> pleasant looking squaws of the Seneca tribe, who
> came and examined me attentively for a short time
> and then went out.   After a few minutes absence
> they returned with my former masters, who gave
> me to them to dispose of. ...
>
> At night we arrived at a small Seneca Indian town
> ... where the two Squaws to whom I belonged re-
> sided.   There we landed, and the Indians went on;
> which was the last I ever saw of them.
>
> Having made fast to the shore, the Squaws left me
> in the canoe while they went to their wigwam ...
> and returned with a suit of Indian clothing, new and
> very clean and nice.   My clothes, though whole and
> good when I was taken, were now torn in pieces,
> so that I was almost naked.   They first undressed
> me and threw my rags into the river, then washed
> me clean and dressed me in the new suit they had
> just brought, in complete Indian style; and then led
> me home and seated me in the center of their wig-
> wam.
>
> I had been in that situation but a few minutes, be-
> fore all the Squaws in the town came in to see me.
> I was soon surrounded by them, and they immedi-

ately set up a most dismal howling, crying bitterly,
and wringing their hands in all the agonies of
grief....

In the course of that ceremony, from mourning they
became serene--joy sparkled in their countenances,
and they seemed to rejoice over me as over a long
lost child.   I was made welcome amongst them as
a sister to the two Squaws before mentioned, and
was called Dickewamis; which being interpreted,
signifies a pretty girl, a handsome girl, or a pleasant, good thing.   That is the name by which I
have ever since been called by the Indians.

I afterwards learned that the ceremony I at that
time passed through, was that of adoption.   The
two squaws had lost a brother in Washington's war,
sometime in the year before, and in consequence
of his death went up to Fort Pitt, on the day on
which I arrived there, in order to receive a prisoner or an enemy's scalp, to supply their loss.

It is a custom of the Indians, when one of their
number is slain or taken prisoner in battle, to give
to the nearest relative to the dead or absent, a
prisoner, if they have chanced to take one, and if
not, to give him the scalp of an enemy.   On the
return of the Indians from conquest, which is always announced by peculiar shoutings, demonstra-
tions of joy, and the exhibition of some trophy of
victory, the mourners come forward and make their
claims.   If they receive a prisoner, it is at their
option either to satiate their vengeance by taking
his life in the most cruel manner they can conceive
of; or, to receive and adopt him into the family,
in the place of him whom they have lost.   All the
prisoners that are taken in battle and carried to
the encampment or town by the Indians, are given
to the bereaved families, till their number is made
good.   And unless the mourners have but just received the news of their bereavement, and are
under the operation of a paroxysm of grief, anger
and revenge; or, unless the prisoner is very old,
sickly, or homely, they generally save him, and
treat him kindly.   But if their mental wound is
fresh, their loss so great that they deem it irre-
parable, or if their prisoner or prisoners do not

meet their approbation, no torture, let it be ever
so cruel, seems sufficient to make them satisfaction. It is family, and not national sacrifices
amongst the Indians, that has given them an indelible stamp as barbarians, and identified their
character with the idea which is generally formed
of unfeeling ferocity, and the most abandoned
cruelty.

It was my happy lot to be accepted for adoption;
and at the time of the ceremony I was received by
the two squaws, to supply the place of their brother
in the family; and I was ever considered and treated by them as a real sister, the same as though I
had been born of their mother.

During my adoption, I sat motionless, nearly terrified to death at the appearance and actions of the
company, expecting every moment to feel their
vengeance, and suffer death on the spot. I was,
however, happily disappointed, when at the close of
the ceremony the company retired, and my sisters
went about employing every means for my consola-
tion and comfort.

Being now settled and provided with a home, I was
employed in nursing the children, and doing light
work about the house. Occasionally I was sent out
with the Indian hunters, when they went but a short
distance, to help them carry their game. My situation was easy; I had no particular hardships to
endure. But still, the recollection of my parents,
my brothers and sisters, my home, and my own
captivity, destroyed my happiness, and made me
constantly solitary, lonesome and gloomy.

My sisters would not allow me to speak English in
their hearing; but remembering the charge that my
dear mother gave me at the time I left her, whenever I chanced to be alone I made a business of
repeating my prayer, catechism, or something I
had learned in order that I might not forget my own
language. By practising in that way I retained it
till I came to Genesee flats, where I soon became
acquainted with English people with whom I have
been almost daily in the habit of conversing.

> My sisters were diligent in teaching me their lan-
> guage; and to their great satisfaction I soon learned
> so that I could understand it readily, and speak it
> fluently.   I was very fortunate in falling into their
> hands; for they were kind good natured women;
> peaceable and mild in their dispositions; temperate
> and decent in their habits, and very tender and
> gentle towards me.   I have great reason to respect
> them, though they have been dead a great number
> of years.

Mary's assimilation soon was far advanced, but it received a temporary reversal the first time she visited a
white settlement.

> About planting time, our Indians all went up to Fort
> Pitt, to make peace with the British, and took me
> with them.   We landed on the opposite side of the
> river from the fort, and encamped for the night.
> Early the next morning the Indians took me over to
> the fort to see the white people that were there. It
> was then that my heart bounded to be liberated from
> the Indians and to be restored to my friends and my
> country.   ... for a long time I brooded the thoughts
> of my miserable situation with almost as much sor-
> row and dejection as I had done those of my first
> sufferings.   Time, the destroyer of every affection,
> wore away my unpleasant feelings, and I became as
> contented as before.

Mary lived contentedly with her Indian sisters until she
reached the age of puberty.   Then she was considered to be
ready for marriage.

> Not long after the Delawares came to live with us,
> at Wiishto, my sisters told me that I must go and
> live with one of them, whose name was Shenin-jee.
> Not daring to cross them, or disobey their com-
> mands, with a great degree of reluctance I went;
> and Sheninjee and I were married according to In-
> dian custom.
>
> Sheninjee was a noble man; large in stature; ele-
> gant in his appearance; generous in his conduct;
> courageous in war; a friend to peace, and a great
> lover of justice.   He supported a degree of dignity
> far above his rank, and merited and received the

confidence and friendship of all the tribes with
whom he was acquainted. Yet, Sheninjee was an
Indian. The idea of spending my days with him,
at first seemed perfectly irreconcilable to my feelings; but his good nature, generosity, tenderness,
and friendship towards me, soon gained my affection; and, strange as it may seem, I loved him!
-- To me he was ever kind in sickness, and always
treated me with gentleness; in fact, he was an
agreeable husband, and a comfortable companion.
We lived happily together till the time of our final
separation....[3]

Captivity of Regina Leininger

Regina Leininger was the daughter of German parents
who came to America about 1742 and settled in the wilderness on the West Branch of the Susquehanna. At the age of
ten she fell into the hands of the Allegheny Indians, along
with her sister Barbara, and remained in captivity for nine
years. When Colonel Bouquet forced the Indians to give up
their captives, Regina was among the bedraggled throng released on the River Muskingum. A few months later she
told her story to the Rev. H. M. Muhlenberg who published
it in the German language. Later the story was translated
into English with the title Regina, the German Captive.

In February, 1765, a widow and her adult daughter
from Rev. Kurtz's congregation came to (see me).
This visit cheered me very much because of the
peculiar circumstances of the case. The widow
spoken of was a native of the old and renowned
Imperial City, Reutlingen, in the Duchy of Wuer-
temburg, and her deceased husband (was born)
about twelve miles from Tuebingen. Before the
war broke out in this country, they, with their
small family of children, came hither and sought a
home in the interior of Pennsylvania about one hundred miles from Philadelphia. The father was already advanced in years and too feeble to endure
hard labor, but endeavored to instruct his children
in the Word of God, because in the thinly settled
country districts few schools are to be found, or
none at all.

In the summer of the year 1755 the English general

Braddock with his army was defeated by the French
and the hostile Indians in the wilderness, because
the English fought according to European methods
and the Indians after the American.   Immediately
thereupon the hostile savages invaded the remote
districts of Pennsylvania and butchered the scattered
and defenceless inhabitants, consisting mostly of
poor German families, dragging their children
through the trackless wilderness into captivity in
their huts and caves.   October 16, 1755, this fate
also befell the above named Christian family, together with a number of our brethren in the faith.
The mother, the widow now still living, and one of
the sons, had gone to a mill a few miles distant,
to secure the grinding of some grain; the father,
together with the oldest son and the two little daughters, remained at home.   The savages suddenly fell
upon them (the house), slaying the father and the
son in their usual barbarous manner.   But they
spared the two little girls, Barbara, twelve years
of age, and Regina, going on ten, bound them, and
dragged them aside into the forest, leaving several
Indians to guard the children.   Within a few days
the others (Indians) continued to bring an additional
number of captive children together.

After the mother and son returned home from the
mill, and found everything burned and in ruins,
they fled further inland (down) to Rev. Pastor
Kurtz's congregation.   The savages now having
brought a good number of children, some of them
set out with them (the children) towards their own
country, not by the usually travelled paths, but
through rough and unsettled sections, so that they
might not be taken from them.   The larger children
were compelled to carry the smaller ones, who
were strapped to their backs.   Now they pursued
their tiresome journey, barefooted, over brushes,
stones, briars, undergrowth (copse), through mire
and swamps.   Some children's feet were worn to
the quick, laying bare the bones and tendons, so
that they thought they must die because of the agony
and the sufferings which they endured.   But they
were urged on mercilessly.   In going through the
brushes and thickets their clothing was torn into
shreds and at last fell from them altogether.   When
they finally reached the country inhabited by the

savages they were divided among them, one being
given to a family here and another to another
several miles further on. It is the custom among
these people, if perchance parents are deprived of
their children in war, that they are replaced by
captives taken by them.

When they had now proceeded about four hundred
English miles the younger ten-year-old daughter,
Regina, was separated from her sister, Barbara,
who had been handed over (to her family) and was
compelled to go more than one hundred miles further, with a two-year-old child, which she was
compelled to carry, strapped to her back.   Finally
Regina also reached the end of her journey, and,
together with the child which she was carrying, was
given over to an old ill-tempered Indian squaw, who
had but one son as her support, to be her slave for
life.   But he (the son) oft times did not return
home for a week or even a longer period, and so
neglected (to provide for) his mother.   In consequence of this the old woman demanded that Regina
should provide sustenance, or be put to death.   The
little helpless infant also clung to Regina and looked
to her for comfort.   They were entirely destitute
of clothing, and the supply of provisions was very
scant.   When the worthless son was not at home
Regina was expected to see to everything if she did
not wish to be scolded and beaten by the old hag
(Woelfin).   It was, therefore, necessary for her to
drag together the wood by which they were warmed.
When the ground was open she looked for and dug
up all manner of wild roots, e. g. , artichokes,
garlic, etc. , and gather the tender bark of trees
and vegetables to preserve the family alive.   When
there was frost in the ground she hunted all kinds
of living creatures, such as wild rats, field mice,
and other animals which she was able to capture,
to satisfy the cravings of hunger.

For more than nine years, she, together with the
other little girl, was compelled to continue in this
mode of life, not knowing whether she should ever
return again.

Through the first terrible calamity, when she was
deprived of her father, mother, brothers and

sister, she was naturally benumbed. In the long
journey, with its attendant cruelties, the deprivation
of all the necessaries and comforts at the hands of
the savages--in continued fears and the very shadow
of death, there was still room for reflection, and
she could not do more than preserve an animal existence. When, however, this miserable mode of
existence had become second nature, and the powers
of the soul were again brought into activity, the
prayers, the passages of Scripture and the sacred
hymns which she had learned from her parents, became her chief delight.   These divine truths were
developed in her soul as a seed which begins to
grow, sending its roots downward and the shoots
upward, when the genial warmth of the sun causes
the earth to produce life.   Thus the Word of God,
learned by her, gradually expended into life, and in
her tribulation brought peace, rest and comfort to
her heart.   The miserable mode of living was a
good assistant and means of restraint to curb the
sinful flesh and its growing desires and the Word of
God implanted in her tender youth could so much the
more readily promote the growth of the inner life.
She stated that during the period of her captivity she
had offered her prayers on bended knees, under the
trees, numberless times, with the child beside her,
uniting in the prayer.   Upon almost every occasion
during the later years she had a faint assurance and
a gleam of hope that she would be released from
captivity and brought back to Christian people.

Among other things the two following hymns had
been and still were a constant source of comfort to
her: viz., 'Jesus Evermore I Love, ' and 'Alone,
and Yet Not Alone Am I. ' When finally, during the
year just passed, the fierce savages were put to
flight, and their homes attacked, especially by the
prudent and brave Colonel Bouquet and his victorious
army, and were compelled to sue for peace, and to
deliver their Christian captives, Regina and her
foster child were released....

From Ft. Pitt the crowd (army) of those rescued
was finally brought into the province of Pennsylvania
to a village named Carlisle. Notice was given in
all the papers that whoever had lost friends, relatives, husband, wife or children, should be on hand

and claim their own (by proper signs). Accordingly
the above-mentioned poor widow with her only yet
remaining son journeyed thither. She asked the
Commissioners for her little daughter, Regina, describing her as she was when between nine and ten
years of age. But she could find no one resembling
her among the crowd. For Regina now was more
than eighteen years of age, fully grown to womanhood, stout, with the bearing of an Indian, and
speaking the language of the savages. The Commissioners asked the mother whether she could not
designate some characteristic by which her daughter
might be known. The mother replied in German:
That her daughter frequently sang the hymn 'Jesus
I Love Evermore, ' and 'Alone, and Yet Not Alone
Am I in My Dread Solitude. '

Hardly had the widow said this when Regina sprang
from among the others and repeated the Creed, the
Lord's Prayer, and the hymns named. Finally the
mother and daughter fell upon each other's neck
shedding tears of joy. The mother with her daughter
whom she had again found hastened to return home.
The little girl for whom Regina had cared, kept
looking on and repeated the things which Regina had
repeated. But no one could be found who recognized
her as their own child. Hence it was thought that
probably her parents had been murdered. But she
was not willing to leave her foster mother and clung
affectionately to Regina so that she could not be
kept back.

This happened at Carlisle, December 31, 1764. In
February, 1765, the widow with her daughter came
to me, saying that since her return her daughter
had continually pled for ... the Bible.... As soon
as she had taken the Bible--with evident pleasure--
I told her to open it and to read to me what first
met her eye. She opened it at the First Chapter
of Tobit and read the second verse intelligibly and
impressively, viz., 'The same was also taken prisoner in the time of Talmanasser (Emmeneser) King
of Assyria, and although prisoner among strangers,
yet did he not depart from the Word of the Lord. '

To me it seemed remarkable that she who had not
seen a German book for nine years, and had not

read a single syllable during that time, yet had not
forgotten how to read, but could do it as well as
when she was taken from her parents and carried
into captivity in her tenth year. She could still
understand German pretty well but could not express herself in it because in regard to matters of
every day life, the Indian language had now become
her mother tongue. [4]

Captivity of Tomassa

Tomassa was born of Mexican parents about the year
1841. She was captured by Comanches at an early age.   In
later life, as a married woman, she attended a school for
Indians on the Comanche-Kiowa Agency near Fort Sill and
described many of her experiences to the teacher, Josiah
Butler.   Born in the Republic of Mexico to parents in comfortable circumstances, she was swept up in one of the frequent Comanche raids which so terrorized that region.   She
was kindly treated by the Comanches and adopted by one of
the Indian families. She lived contentedly with the Comanches
for several years.   Then, along with other captive children,
she was ransomed by the Mexican Government.

Unable to recall her family name or where she had
come from, she was not reclaimed by her relatives.   Also
unclaimed was a boy a little older than Tomassa and the two
of them were turned over as servants to a wealthy family.
Their new life of drudgery seeming less attractive to the
children than the captivity from which they had been redeemed, they decided to run away at the first opportunity and
rejoin the tribe.   Over a period of time they accumulated a
store of provisions and stole away from the hacienda one
night, during a celebration.   Helping themselves to a horse,
they struck out toward the Rio Grande with only the North
Star as a guide.   After traveling hundreds of miles their
food supply gave out and they averted starvation by killing
their horse and drying the meat in Indian fashion.   As they
still had many miles of desert and mountains to cross on
foot they used the hide to make extra moccasins.   Finally
they managed to locate their Comanche families, a rather
remarkable feat of pathfinding and endurance for children
ten to twelve years of age.

And so she was happy to again take up life in the
lodge of her Comanche foster mother, with whom

she lived until she grew to womanhood, when she
married the white trader and ranchman, Joseph
Chandler, who was many years her senior.   A
daughter and three sons were born of this marriage.
Although she was a married woman and the mother
of several children, she entered the Comanche
school at the Fort Sill Agency, when it was first
opened by Josiah Butler, to be not only a pupil but
also the teacher's interpreter.   After her husband's
death, she married George Conover, to whom three
sons were born.   Her children and grandchildren
all reside in the vicinity of Anadarko, where she
died, December 6, 1900, aged about fifty-five
years. [5]

Another official who reported a part of Tomassa's
story and throws some light on the assimilation process was
the famous Indian agent, Lawrie Tatum.   He stated that she
had been promised in marriage to an Indian named Blue Leggings but insisted on marrying Chandler instead.   When the
Indian declined to give her up she retorted that he would
have to kill her in order to take her.   Finally he sold
Chandler his rights to the girl for three dollars and a crow-
ing chicken. [6]

After her marriage to Chandler, Tomassa lived on
cattle ranches in Texas and the Indian Territory.   She
adopted many of the ways of white civilization and tried to
help Indians follow her example.   Frequently she warned
white people of impending raids.   Once she saved the lives
of two Mexican captives by hiding them under the floor of
her house. [7]

Captivity of Clinton Smith

Clinton Smith, the eleven-year-old son of an Anglo-
Saxon ranch family, was captured by Comanche Indians near
Dripping Springs, Texas on March 3, 1869.   His younger
brother, Jeff, was taken at the same time.   Clinton remained
in captivity almost four years and Jeff was held a year or
two longer.   Both boys became thoroughly Indianized.   After
reluctantly returning to their family they experienced a great
deal of difficulty in readjusting to the white man's way of life.
Eventually they married and became respected ranchers, but
they retained strong affection for their Indian friends.   Both
of them have written accounts of their experiences which

reveal some facets of the assimilation process.

The band which captured the Smith boys contained both
Comanches and Lipans.   They camped for the night on the
Perdenales River and the boys tried to escape, only to be
overtaken almost immediately.   The next day the Texas
Rangers took up their trail and pursued them closely for two
hundred miles but turned back after the Indians scattered and
fired the grass.

When the boys reached the Comanche village they
were adopted into the tribe.   Not long afterwards, the Comanches attacked a wagon train and massacred every man,
woman, and child.   During the battle Clinton was wounded
by a stray bullet.   By the spring of 1870, Clinton was already becoming assimilated even though he had been in captivity only a year.   At that time he went on his first raid
into Texas.   He recalled:

> We were all painted up, and no one could have told
> me from an Indian boy.   We came to a ranch at
> which there was no one except a woman and two
> little children.   Two horses were tied to the gate.
> We got them, and tried to get the woman, but she
> put up a desperate fight.   The Indians shot the door
> full of arrows, and the woman shot the chief in the
> neck so we left her alone.
>
> We then moved on towards Fort Sill, where the
> Indians could get more guns and ammunition. . . .
> While in camp waiting for the return of those who
> went to the fort, the Indians had all kinds of
> sports.   The Indian boys and I would go in bathing
> every day, run horse races, rope buffalo calves
> and ride them, and take wild horses out into deep
> sand and ride them.   I was now pretty well Indi-
> anized. . . .

During their wanderings, the band fell in with Geronimo's Apaches and the fierce Chiricahua traded the Comanches
a horse and arms and ammunition for Jeff.   They tied the
youngster so that he could not move and branded him like a
calf.   In February 1871 the tribes went their separate ways
and the boys parted with great sorrow.

In the spring of 1871 Clinton went on a raid against
the settlements.   By this time he had become completely

Indianized. "As I grew older, " he recalled, "my chief
pushed me to the front with the warriors, and it seemed the
longer I stayed with them the more fights they had, and I
was forced to do my share of fighting. "

Once he went on a horse stealing raid right into a
Texas town. "I saw three or four lamps burning in little
homes in that town, and perhaps I should have made an attempt to escape at that time from the Indians, but I had been
with them for some time and had become so attached to my
chief and members of the tribe I could not muster courage
enough to try to make my get-away. My association with
them for so long had impressed me with the feeling that I
could never make a successful attempt to escape, and the desire to do so had about subsided away. I considered myself
an Indian, and an Indian I would be. "

At this time Clinton was about thirteen years old. He
met other white captives and all of the boys of that age were
compelled to go on raids. At first they were used to hold
the horses. After some experience they became full-fledged
warriors.

A year or two later they met the Apaches and Clinton
saw Jeff again. By this time the younger brother had almost
entirely forgotten the English language. He did not seem to
remember who he was but he remembered Clinton.

One of Clinton's fellow captives was Adolph Korn, a
German boy who had been held for eight or nine years. He
was one of the most skillful warriors in the band. Once they
made a night foray into a little town. Although lights were
still burning and the Indians were afraid to follow, Adolph and
Clinton went into the stables and led the horses out one by
one. The next day the raiders killed two white men who were
quarrying rock for a chimney near Fort Concho.

On September 20, 1872, General Ranald McKenzie
caught up with the Comanches near the Red River and the
surprised Indians fled in all directions. But there was one
warrior who did not run. He was the German boy, Adolph
Korn. He hid in the brush and shot an arrow through the
lapel of General McKenzie's coat, narrowly missing the skin.
In the attack many squaws and Indian children were killed and
Clinton burned with hatred against his own race. "After what
I had seen that day I was mad all over, and was willing to
risk anything to get even with the soldiers, " he recalled.

That night he participated in a desperate attack on the troops which permitted many of the prisoners to escape. During the next few months the Comanches hit the frontier hard. Clinton saw so many people killed that he "looked upon it as ... of no more consequence than killing a cow. "

Pressure from troops finally forced the band onto the reservation at Fort Sill. The white captives were taken to the fort and released. Clinton was given the opportunity to return to the white people but he refused. He was forcibly delivered to the fort by some of the Indians, along with eight other captives, one of whom was a sixteen-year-old girl with a half-Indian baby. They were locked in the guard house to prevent their running away until their relatives arrived to reclaim them. The girl had forgotten her name and no one ever arrived to reclaim her.

Clinton Smith and Adolph Korn were sent to San Antonio under troop escort. When they made camp the first night the boys tried to steal horses and escape but were discovered and closely guarded during the rest of the trip. They were delivered to Adolph Korn's father, the owner of the largest candy store in San Antonio. The German boy was absolutely uncontrollable. He kept getting into trouble and urged Clinton to run away with him. He was sixteen years old and had been with the Indians half of his life. A short time after his release he stole a horse and returned to the Comanches.

Clinton Smith, too, found it difficult to resume life as a white boy. After his younger brother, Jeff, was reclaimed from Geronimo the two boys were almost impossible to control. "But we were happy in each other's company, " he wrote, "and our family bestowed every kindness and sympathy upon us, until the gentle refining influence of home life began to have its effect and we became civilized again. "

"I have been asked many times, " Clinton Smith wrote, "'Did you ever kill anybody while you were with the Indians?' When asked this question I always hang my head and do not reply.... It must be remembered that I was just a mere boy, and that I had, without choice, absorbed the customs and manners of a savage tribe. "[8]

Captivity of Herman Lehmann

Herman Lehmann was born of German parents on
June 5, 1859. He was captured by Apaches in May, 1870 in
Gillespie County, Texas, and lived with them four years.
Then he killed an Apache medicine man, fled to the Comanches, and was adopted into that tribe. He remained with
the Comanches until he was restored to the whites, a fully
grown man and a warrior. During his captivity he had forgotten his own language and had become completely Indianized.

Some time after his redemption, Lehmann told his
story to J. Marvin Hunter, editor and publisher of Frontier
Times. It is one of the most interesting of captivity narratives, for Lehmann probably participated in as many raids
against the whites as did any other Indianized Texas captive.

Upon reaching the Apache village, Herman withstood
torture so bravely that the Indians considered him warrior
timber. Once he escaped but was recaptured and whipped.
"After this," he wrote, "a boy accompanied me and kept me
from being so lonesome. He taught me their language,
showed me how to fix arrows and make bows. We herded
the horses and I waited on my master, Carnoviste, the chief;
he stole me, so I belonged to him. I would get his horse,
bring his food, light his pipe, bathe his feet, paint his skin,
tighten the spikes on his arrows, catch lice on his head and
body, and attend to what other chores he required, some not
decent to put in this book.

"... according to tribal custom, I belonged to Carnoviste, and was called his son. He gave me an Indian name,
En Da, meaning 'white boy.' His squaw, Laughing Eyes,
was very good to me and treated me as her own. At that
time she had no child of her own and she lavished affection
upon me, and in my childish way I returned her caresses."

When he had been with the Apaches about a year he
participated in the first of many raids which he describes in
the book. They found a family traveling in a wagon and
quickly killed and scalped the parents and a baby. A boy of
six and a girl of eight were taken prisoner, but the children
refused to eat and cried so much that the Indians killed them
and hung their bodies on a tree as food for the vultures.

"I hesitate to recite these revolting crimes," Lehmann
wrote, "but they were true instances of the savagery in

which I was engulfed through no choice of my own...."

Gradually he began to regard the Indians as his own
people and whites as enemies.   Once on a raid his band
captured a white boy.   "We kept that boy about a year," he
recalled, "but as he would not take to our ways, we traded
him to some Mexicans."

When the Apaches were driven onto the reservation,
only two years after his capture, he hid from the soldiers.
A short time later, during a fight with Texas Rangers, he
was recognized as white and had only to give himself up.   A
little Mexican captive ran toward the Rangers with his hands
lifted high, but Lehmann fought them until his horse was
killed, pinning him to the ground.   When the Rangers rode
up he feigned death.   In a moment they left in pursuit of the
Indians.   Then he freed himself and hid in the brush, finally
walking three hundred miles and almost starving to death in
order to rejoin the tribe.

When he had been with the Indians five years he killed
a medicine man and fled from the Apaches to join the Comanches.   "I told them ... that I was a white man by birth
but an Indian by adoption; that I loved the Indian and hated
the white man; that on my shield were the scalps of whites
whom I had killed in battle, and that I was regarded by my
race as a mortal enemy; ... that I wanted to become a Comanche, and dwell with them and forever make war on the
Apaches and white people."

Lehmann was adopted by a Comanche family and remained with the tribe four years, raiding most of the time.
He killed settlers and buffalo hunters and collected their
scalps.

Like many other captives, Lehmann became Indianized
more completely as a result of brutality by white soldiers
against his adopted people.   While the warriors were away
on a horse stealing raid the Indian camp was attacked by
U. S. Cavalry and Tonkaway Scouts.   Five squaws were killed
and others and their children captured.   A beautiful Indian
maiden named Nooki was horribly mutilated and disemboweled.

"We soon found our scattered women and children and
old men," wrote Lehmann, "and heard the sad details of the
attack, and our rage knew no bounds.   Five of our women

and several children were captives in the hands of the soldiers. In our council we swore to take ten captive white
women and twice as many white children, and to avenge the
death of our squaws, especially Nooki; we vowed to kill a
white woman for each year of her age (she was about 18
years old), and that we would disembowel every one we
killed. "

Gradually the soldiers gained control over the South
Plains and white buffalo hunters eliminated the Indians' food
supply. Finally Quanah Parker, son of the famous captive,
Cynthia Ann, led the Comanches to the reservation. Lehmann was one of the last to go in and he spent his final
years among the Indians as an adopted member of Quanah's
family. "Quanah told me my mother and folks were still
alive, and asked me if I wanted to go to them, " he recalled.
"I told him no; that the Indians were my people.... "

Finally, under Quanah's persuasion, he agreed to go
home. He made the trip from Fort Sill, Oklahoma, to Loyal
Valley, Texas, under military guard. During his first year
of redemption he was watched constantly to prevent his running away. But in time he ceased longing for the wild Comanche ways, settled down with a wife, and raised a family.[9]

Captivity of Andres Martinez

Andres Martinez, a Mexican-American, was captured
by Mescalero Apaches on October 6, 1866, near Las Vegas,
New Mexico. He was about eight years old when taken and
he remained in captivity almost twenty years. After hostilities ended he returned to his Mexican family, but in a short
time he decided that his place was with the Indians and he
went back to the reservation. Eventually he became an interpreter and teacher in a mission school. At that time he
told the story of his captivity to the Rev. J. J. Methvin,
missionary to the wild tribes in the Indian Territory.

Andres was given to his captor's wife. He carried
wood and water and herded the horses. In a short time,
however, he was traded to another band for a supply of
liquor. His new masters beat and abused him until he was
rescued by two Kiowa warriors. One of them was a Mexican
who had been captured many years earlier and raised as an
Indian. The other warrior, Heap-o'-Bears, adopted him as
a son. The Kiowas treated him kindly.

Such a change from oppression and cruelty, to one
of comfort and kindness, made Andres very grateful and took his mind at last from thoughts of
home. In a few days his head was well and the
great sores on his body had healed up, and Andres
was happy and contented with his new friends.

The Kiowas returned to their homeland on the Wichita,
far to the east. Andres adopted the Kiowa life style rapidly.
When Heap-o'-Bears returned from a raid with two scalps,
Andres joined in the scalp dance with wild delight. "By the
spring of 1869 Andres had become a veritable Indian with but
little trace of civilized life left in him. He had learned
many things of the Indian life and accepted them all. "

By 1871 Andres had decided to become a great war
chief and asked permission to go on a raid.

"Andele, " said Napawat, "you are too young for war."

"No, no, " he answered, "I want to go, I know I can
scalp the enemy. My medicine is strong. "

The Kiowas attacked the home of a Texas Ranger and
he stood them off with rifle fire. Andres did not obtain a
scalp but he did succeed in stealing the Ranger's mule.

When Andres became a young man he married a Kiowa
girl but she ran away with another Indian. In a short time
he married again but put her away as they did not get along.
A year later he married a third time and lived happily with
her until she died.

After Andres had lived as an Indian for almost twenty
years he decided to change his way of life and applied to the
agent for work. He received training as a blacksmith and
his contacts with whites led him to recall the circumstances
of his early life. He went home to New Mexico for four
years and then returned to the Indians as "his interests were
all identified with the Kiowas, and he had learned to love
them. "[10]

Conclusions

Based on the evidence gleaned from the narratives
presented above, is it possible to reach conclusions regard-

ing the importance of national origin in affecting the assimilation of captives?   Among the males, all three were captured during childhood in the same general region and in
approximately the same period of frontier history.   All three
were treated with great cruelty at first, then were adopted
into a tribe and regarded almost as though they were Indians
by birth.   All three became greatly Indianized, went on raids
against white people, and were reluctant to return to their
original families.   Their experiences have so much in common that it is difficult to discover significant differences
which could be attributed to pre-captivity cultural influences.
Moreover, the study of many additional narratives of captivity
does not provide conclusive evidence that national origins
affected assimilation.

Jeff Smith, Comanche and Apache captive, remarked
that the Indians preferred Mexican captives "because when
they brought them in they could raise them up and no one
could tell them from full blood Indians."[11]   Certainly in the
Southwest, Mexican captives outnumbered those of Anglo-
American or German stock.   But this is evidence, only, that
Mexican captives were easier to obtain.   It does not neces-
sarily follow that they were easier to Indianize.   Swanton
has written that "It may very properly be objected that as
most Mexicans themselves have Indian blood the testimony of
Mexican captives is inconclusive."   He could find no evidence, however, that they were more easily assimilated than
others.[12]

As a matter of fact, Andres Martinez seems to have
been less thoroughly Indianized than either Clinton Smith or
Herman Lehmann.   In spite of the fact that he lived longer
with the Indians than either Smith or Lehmann, he was the
only one of the three who voluntarily returned to his own
people.   It is true that he eventually rejoined the Indians but
he became an interpreter and teacher and helped his adopted
people to learn the white man's ways.

The male captives mentioned in the foregoing narratives who became the fiercest warriors were Herman Lehmann and Adolph Korn, both German-Americans.   Is there
any basis for concluding, therefore, that German-American
children were more readily assimilated than captives of other
origins?   In the Southwest, other sons of German emigrants
became noted warriors.   Rudolph Fischer was a Comanche
captive for several years and after being restored to his
parents he took the first opportunity to run away and rejoin

his captors. [13]   Another noted warrior was known only as
Kiowa Dutch.   A big, blond youth, he was notorious on the
Texas frontier as he raided with the predatory chief, Satanta,
and cursed white people in their own language while doing
his best to kill them. [14]

When one considers the narratives of the female captives, however, it is found that the German-American, Regina Leininger, was the least assimilated of the three.   While
Mary Jemison was becoming the contented wife of an Indian,
Regina was praying in German so that she would not lose
command of her native language.   Moreover, Regina's sister,
Barbara, was successful in resisting assimilation.   She held
onto the hope of escape and when the opportunity arose she
risked death by torture to traverse hundreds of miles of
wilderness to return to civilization. [15]   It is of interest to
note that of the two girls surrendered to Bouquet who slipped
away almost immediately to rejoin the Indians, one was of
English and the other of German extraction.

When other cultural groups are considered, no clearer
picture of the relationship between national origin and ease of
assimilation emerges.   In the earliest period of exploration
and colonization, a considerable number of Spaniards fell
into the hands of the Indians.   Among the earliest of these
was Juan Ortiz, captured in Florida in 1529, who lived with
the Indians for eleven years.   When white men returned to
Florida he had almost forgotten his native language. [16]
Cabeza de Vaca and the other survivors of the Narváez Expedition were held in captivity by various tribes in Texas and
Mexico but never gave up hope of reaching their countrymen.
They learned many of the ways of the Indians and exerted
great influence over some of the tribes but were never content to remain with any of them. [17]   On the other hand, when
several children of unmixed Castilian ancestry were captured
in Chihuahua, Mexico, about 1810, by Kiowas or Comanches,
they became readily assimilated.   The girls married Indians
and their descendants became prominent warriors. [18]

Generally speaking, the French got along better with
Indians than did the peoples of other European nations.   In
Canada the coureurs de bois lived among the tribes and as-
sumed some Indian traits but remained essentially Frenchmen.   Except for the Iroquois, most tribes participating in
the colonial wars were allies of the French.   Consequently
the French received many English captives, while comparatively few of them became captives themselves.   When the

Iroquois made prisoners of French children, however, the
assimilation process went on much the same as it did with
children of other national origins. The narrative of Pierre
Esprit Radisson, which will be included in a later chapter,
is one of the most revealing in regard to the Indianization
process.

        One final racial group, the Negro, remains to be con-
sidered. Here, unfortunately, primary source materials are
lacking. Vail records only two narratives of captivity by
blacks among the hundreds listed in his bibliography, and in
neither case was the captive held long enough to be assimilated. [19] Hundreds of Negroes lived with Indians in the South,
but most of them were runaway slaves or their descendants
who joined the tribe voluntarily. [20] In Florida, particularly,
blacks became tribal leaders and their life style was much
the same as that of their Seminole Indian associates. In
Ohio and Kentucky the Shawnees and Wyandots held a few
black captives who had become greatly assimilated although
they retained the use of English well enough to serve as in-
terpreters. [21] In Texas and the Southwest, Indians developed
the practice of stealing slaves for ransom or selling them to
slave traders in Arkansas and the Indian Territory. [22] There
was at least one black child with Geronimo's Apache raiders
at the time of his final surrender, [23] but if Negro captives
west of the Mississippi lived long enough with the Indians to
become assimilated, little mention of the fact appears in
original narratives of that region.

        In attempting to ascertain the importance of race and
national origins in facilitating or retarding Indianization, a
chart has been prepared showing the estimated degree of
assimilation of captives of various ethnic stocks. It is difficult, of course, to arrive at accurate estimates because information is scanty in a majority of cases. Further complicating the matter is the problem of interpreting such facts
as are known in terms of degree of assimilation. Learning
the Indian language was a definite sign of the beginning of
assimilation, even for those who longed to return to their
white families. Failure to attempt to escape was no proof
of Indianization, however, for fear may have overridden a
cherished hope to return. On the other hand, repeated escape attempts present unmistakable evidence of resistance to
assimilation. Attaining skill in Indian activities, such as the
use of the bow and arrow, indicates some coming to terms
with the new way of life, but it does not preclude the possibility that the captive would have preferred to escape if given

NAME	NATIONAL ORIGIN	ASSIMILATION
Armstrong, Thomas	Anglo-American	100%
Asu-que-ti	Mexican	100
Aw-i	Mexican	100
Durgan, Millie	Anglo-American	100
Fischer, Rudolph	German-American	100
French, Abigail	Anglo-American	100
Hurst, Hanno	Anglo-American	100
Korn, Adolph	German-American	100
Mo-Keen	Mexican	100
Saenz, Bernardino	Mexican	100
Hoah-Wah	Mexican	95
Kiowa Dutch	German-American	95
Long Horn	Mexican	95
M'Cullough, John	Anglo-American	95
Mak-suh	Mexican	95
Smith, Jeff	Anglo-American	95
Brayton, Matthew	Anglo-American	90
Brown, Adam	Anglo-American	90
Friend, Temple	Anglo-American	90
M'Allum, Dan	Anglo-American	90
Moxie, John Valentine	Anglo-American	90
Waggoner, Peter	Anglo-American	90
McLennan, John	Anglo-American	85
Hunter, John	Anglo-American	80
Kellogg, Rebecca	Anglo-American	80
Malone, Rachel	Anglo-American	75
Carter, Mercy	Anglo-American	65
Aes-nap	Mexican	60
Gill, Samuel	Anglo-American	60
Longley, John	Anglo-American	60
Searls, Elisha	Anglo-American	60
Boyd, Thomas	Anglo-American	55
Lyons, Warren	Anglo-American	50
Metzger, Anna	German-American	50
Pres-lean-no	Mexican	50
Sale-beal	Mexican	50
Babb, T. A.	Anglo-American	45
Door, Jonathan	Anglo-American	45
Gonzales, Levando	Mexican	45
Radisson, Pierre Esprit	French-American	45
Girty, Simon	Anglo-American	40
Moore, James	Anglo-American	25
Leininger, Barbara	German-American	20
Smith, James	Anglo-American	20

NAME	NATIONAL ORIGIN	ASSIMILATION
Gibson, Hugh	Anglo-American	15
Oatman, Olive	Anglo-American	15
Gyles, John	Anglo-American	10
Bradley, Isaac	Anglo-American	5
Diaz, Martina	Mexican	5
Plummer, Rachel	Anglo-American	0

the opportunity. Marrying an Indian would appear to provide proof of assimilation if one could be sure that the captive submitted voluntarily to the association. Even raids against white settlements do not present positive proof of Indianization if one accepts the defense presented by some redeemed captives that they were compelled to go along. The most reliable evidence of assimilation is the rejection of an opportunity to return in safety to the white family, but even here the element of shame as a deterrent must be considered.

In spite of these problems it is believed that when a sufficient number of cases are considered it is possible to determine whether or not a significant correlation exists between national origin and degree of assimilation (shown on the chart as a percentage figure).

In attempting to ascertain the importance of race and national origins in facilitating or retarding Indianization, no significant correlation was found in a sample of more than fifty case studies. It is tentatively concluded, therefore, that racial or national origins are of little or no importance in affecting assimilation. Attention will be focused upon other factors in attempting to learn why one captive accepted life as an Indian while another rejected every phase of the culture of his captors.

Notes

1. C. Rister, Border Captives, 9, 58-59. Copyright 1940 by the University of Oklahoma Press.

2. Thomas Fitzpatrick, Report, as quoted in James Mooney, "Calendar History of the Kiowa Indians," Bureau of American Ethnology Annual Report, 17th. (Washington, 1898), 174.

3. Mary Jemison, A Narrative of the Life of Mrs. Mary Jemison. (New York, 1929), 40-53.

4. Henry Melchior Muhlenberg, "Regina, the German Captive," in Pennsylvania German Society Proceedings, XV (1906), 82-89.

5. Josiah Butler, "Pioneer School Teaching at the Comanche-Kiowa Agency School, 1870-03," in Chronicles of Oklahoma, VI (1928), 499-500.

6. Lawrie Tatum, Our Red Brothers. (Philadelphia, 1899), 60-61.

7. Thomas C. Battey, The Life and Adventures of a Quaker Among the Indians. (Boston, 1875), 155-56.

8. Clinton L. Smith, The Boy Captives. (Hackberry, Texas, 1927).

9. Herman Lehmann, Nine Years With the Indians. (Austin, 1927).

10. J. J. Methvin, Andele, or the Mexican-Kiowa Captive. (Louisville, 1899).

11. Smith, The Boy Captives, 182.

12. Swanton, "Notes on the Mental Assimilation of Races," 497.

13. Lehmann, Nine Years With the Indians, 217.

14. Clarence Wharton, Satanta. (Dallas, 1935), 14, 59.

15. Barbara Leininger, "The Narrative of Marie LeRoy and Barbara Leininger," in Pennsylvania German Society Proceedings, XV (1906), 109-23.

16. Garcilaso de la Vega, The Florida of the Inca. (Austin, 1951), 63-79.

17. Núñez Cabeza de Vaca, Álvar, The Journey of Álvar Núñez Cabeza de Vaca. (Chicago, 1964).

18. Hugh D. Corwin, Comanche and Kiowa Captives in Oklahoma and Texas. (Lawton, Oklahoma, 1959), 14-17.

19.   Vail, Voice of the Old Frontier, 271-72.

20.   Kenneth W. Porter, "Relations Between Negroes and
      Indians, " in Journal of Negro History, XVII (1932),
      321-25.

21.   John Bakeless, Daniel Boone.   (New York, 1939), 218;
      James B. Finley, Life Among the Indians.   (Cincin-
      nati, n. d.), 239-42.

22.   Kenneth W. Porter, "Indians and Negroes on the Texas
      Frontier, " in Journal of Negro History, XLI (1956),
      287.

23.   Paul I. Wellman, Death on Horseback.   (Philadelphia,
      1947), caption of photograph between p. 324 and 325.

Chapter 5

TREATMENT OF CAPTIVES
IN THE EASTERN WOODLANDS

Having concluded that ease of assimilation of captives
was little affected by their cultural origins, is it possible to
determine whether the course of Indianization differed significantly among captives held in varying Indian culture areas?
Spencer and Jennings divide the present United States into
five major native American culture areas: Ultra-Mississippi
(mainly east of the Mississippi River with a westward exten-
sion along the Gulf Coast); Plains; Greater Southwest; West
(containing sub-areas in the Great Basin, Plateau, and California); and Northwest Coast (which extends from northern
California to Alaska). [1]

White captive-taking was concentrated in the first
three of these areas and the narratives of a representative
number of captives held there will be presented in search of
clues as to whether the treatment of prisoners differed suf-
ficiently to facilitate or retard the rate of assimilation. Few
narratives of captives taken on the Northwest Coast are
available, but one excellent account is presented in Chapter
6. One brief narrative from the West culture area, also,
is included, as it presents an interesting account of the
course of assimilation, though the narrator seems to have
gone with the Indians voluntarily. In the summary which follows the narratives, answers are sought to the following
questions: (1) How much did treatment of white captives vary
among culture groups? (2) Did variations in treatment affect
assimilation?

Captivity of Juan Ortiz

Juan Ortiz was born in Seville, Spain. He was eighteen years old when he accompanied the Narváez Expedition
to Florida and with three companions fell into the hands of
the Timucua tribe in 1528. One of the first Europeans ever
captured by North American Indians, he remained with them

51

twelve years before being rescued by the DeSoto Expedition.

Chief Hirrihigua, whose mother had been murdered
while his nose was being cut off by members of the Narváez
Expedition, was eager for revenge. He kept Ortiz under
guard while compelling the other Spanish captives to run
around the plaza, warriors winging arrows at them until they
succumbed. Then the chief ordered Ortiz out to suffer the
same fate, but his wife and daughters begged for the boy's
life, pointing out that he had had no part in the atrocities.
Hirrihigua agreed with great reluctance to spare Juan's life,
but made him a slave.

Juan was treated cruelly as long as he remained in
Hirrihigua's hands. Forced to guard the tribal burying
grounds against wild animals every night, he was compelled
on feast days to run continuously in the plaza for the entire
day. He wished many times that he had died with his companions.

Convinced finally that Ortiz would survive his harsh
treatment, Hirrihigua determined to torture him to death.

> So to finish with the youth he gave the order on a
> certain feast day to kindle a great fire in the center
> of the plaza, and when he saw many live coals
> made, he commanded that they be spread out and
> that over them there be placed a grill-like wooden
> structure which stood a yard above the ground, and
> upon which they should put his captive in order to
> roast him alive. Thus it was done, and here the
> poor Spaniard, after being tied to the grill, lay
> stretched out on one side for a long time. But at
> the shrieks of the miserable youth, the wife and
> daughters of the Cacique rushed up, and, pleading
> with their lord and even scolding him for his
> cruelty, removed the boy from the fire, not, how-
> ever, before he was half-baked and blisters that
> looked like halves of oranges had formed on one of
> his sides. Some of these blisters burst and much
> blood ran from them, so that they were painful to
> behold. Hirrihigua overlooked what his wife and
> daughters were doing because they were women
> whom he loved deeply, and possibly also because
> he wanted someone on whom he later might vent his
> wrath and exercise his vengeance.

Ortiz had many other occasions to be grateful to the chief's wife and, especially, to his eldest daughter. Finally, when Hirrihigua determined once more to put him to death, the young Indian woman helped him escape to a village ruled by one Mucozo, a chief who desired to marry her. As a favor to the girl, Mucozo treated Ortiz kindly, risking war with Hirrihigua and even giving up his hopes for the marriage as a result of his refusal to deliver up the captive. Garcilaso de la Vega, historian of the DeSoto Expedition, observed that

> when one has considered well the circumstances of this Indian's valiant deed, the people for whom and against whom it was performed, and even the great amount he was willing to forego and forfeit, even proceeding contrary to his own love and desire by denying the aid and favor asked of and promised by him, it will be seen that he was born with a most generous and heroic spirit and did not deserve to have come into the world and lived in the barbarous paganism of Florida.

After eight years with Mucozo, Ortiz became greatly assimilated. When DeSoto arrived in Florida, the kindly chief sent Ortiz to him as a messenger of peace and to rejoin his countrymen. "Rejoicing over this fortunate news ... Ortiz expressed great pleasure that a time and occasion should have arisen wherein he might render service for the mercy and benefits bestowed upon him...." He was very nearly slain by the Spaniards who mistook him for an Indian, for he had forgotten their language and made himself known as a Christian by giving the sign of the cross.[2]

It is probable that this early sixteenth-century captive was the first European to become substantially Indianized. Had the DeSoto expedition not passed his way he probably would have become completely assimilated.

Captivity of Elizabeth Hanson

Among many women captured in New England by Canadian Indians was Mrs. Elizabeth Hanson, a young New Hampshire housewife. Taken captive on June 27, 1724, she was held by the Indians and French for about a year. Her narrative provides one of the best insights into the capriciousness of Indians, a trait which frequently determined whether a captive died a fiery death or lived as a cherished adopted relative:

... two of them came in upon us, and then eleven
more, all naked, with their guns and tomahawks,
and in a great fury killed one child immediately, as
soon as they entered the door, thinking thereby to
strike in us the greater terror, and to make us
more fearful of them. After which, in like fury,
the captain came up to me; but at my request he
gave me quarter. There were with me our servant
and six of our children; two of the little ones being
at play about the orchard, and my youngest child,
but fourteen days old....

... two of my younger children, one six, and the
other four years old, came in sight, and being under
a great surprise, cried aloud, upon which one of
the Indians running to them, took them under the
arms, and brought them to us. My maid prevailed
with the biggest to be quiet and still; but the other
could by no means be prevailed with, but continued
shrieking and crying very much, and the Indians, to
ease themselves of the noise, and to prevent the
danger of a discovery that might arise from it, immediately, before my face, knocked his brains out.

... having killed two of my children, they scalped
them ... and then put forward to leave the house
in great haste, without doing any other spoil than
taking what they had packed together, with myself
and little babe, fourteen days old, the boy six
years, and two daughters, the one about fourteen
and the other about sixteen years, with my servant....

In this condition aforesaid we left the house, each
Indian having something; and I with my babe and
three children that could go of themselves. The
captain, though he had as great a load as he could
well carry, and was helped up with it, did, for all
that, carry my babe for me in his arms, which I
took to be a favor from him. Thus we went through
several swamps and some brooks, they carefully
avoiding all paths of any track like a road, lest by
our footsteps we should be followed.

... for twenty-six days, day by day we travelled
very hard, sometimes a little by water, over lakes
and ponds; and in this journey we went up some

high mountains, so steep that I was forced to creep
up on my hands and knees; under which difficulty,
the Indian, my master, would mostly carry my babe
for me, which I took as a great favor of God, that
his heart was so tenderly inclined to assist me,
though he had, as it is said, a very heavy burden
of his own; nay he would sometimes take my very
blanket, so that I had nothing to do but to take my
little boy by the hand for his help, and assist him
as well as I could, taking him up in my arms a
little at times, because so small; and when we came
to very bad places, he would lend me his hand, or
coming behind, would push me before him; in all
which, he showed some humanity and civility, more
than I could have expected: for which privilege I
was secretly thankful to God, as the moving cause
thereof.

At last the captives reached the Indian village. There
the older children were sent away to other towns, leaving
only the baby and small boy with the distraught mother. At
that time the captor who had shown not a little compassion
during their sufferings, had a change of attitude.

We had not been long at home ere my master went
a hunting, and was absent about a week, he order-
ing me in his absence to get in wood, gather nuts,
&c. I was very diligent cutting the wood and put-
ting it in order, not having very far to carry it.
But when he returned, having got no prey, he was
very much out of humor, and the disappointment
was so great that he could not forbear revenging it
on us poor captives. However, he allowed me a
little boiled corn for myself and child, but with a
very angry look threw a stick or corn cob at me
with such violence as did bespeak he grudged our
eating. At this his squaw and daughter broke out
into a great crying. This made me fear mischief
was hatching against us. I immediately went out of
his presence into another wigwam; upon which he
came after me, and in a great fury tore my blanket
off my back, and took my little boy from me, and
struck him down as he went along before him; but
the poor child not being hurt, only frightened in the
fall, started up and ran away without crying. Then
the Indian, my master, left me; but his wife's
mother came and sat down by me, and told me I

must sleep there that night. She then going from
me a little time, came back with a small skin to
cover my feet withal, informing me that my master
intended now to kill us, and I, being desirous to
know the reason, expostulated, that in his absence
I had been diligent to do as I was ordered by him.
Thus as well as I could I made her sensible, how
unreasonable he was. Now, though she could not
understand me, nor I her, but by signs, we rea-
soned as well as we could. She therefore made
signs that I must die, advising me, by pointing up
with her fingers, in her way, to pray to God, en-
deavoring by her signs and tears to instruct me in
that which was most needful, viz. to prepare for
death, which now threatened me: the poor old
squaw was so very kind and tender, that she would
not leave me all the night, but laid herself down at
my feet, designing what she could to assuage her
son-in-law's wrath, who had conceived evil against
me, chiefly, as I understood, because the want of
victuals urged him to it. My rest was little this
night, my poor babe sleeping sweetly by me.

But once again the Indian had a change of heart. He
decided to sell the captives rather than kill them.

My master being, as I suppose, weary to keep us,
was willing to make what he could of our ransom;
therefore, he went further towards the French, and
left his family in this place, where they had a
great dance, sundry other Indians coming to our
people. This held some time, and while they were
in it, I got out of their way in a corner of the
wigwam as well (as) I could; but every time they
came by me in their dancing, they would bow my
head towards the ground, and frequently kick me
with as great fury as they could bear, being sundry
of them barefoot, and others having Indian mocko-
sons. This dance held some time, and they made,
in their manner, great rejoicings and noise.

It was not many days ere my master returned from
the French; but he was in such a humor when he
came back, he would not suffer me in his presence.
Therefore I had a little shelter made with some
boughs, they having digged through the snow to the
ground, it being pretty deep. In this hole I and my

children were put to lodge; the weather being very
sharp, with hard frost, in the month called January, made it more tedious to me and my children.
Our stay was not long in this place before he took
me to the French, in order for a chapman. When
we came among them I was exposed for sale, and
he asked for me 800 livres.   But this chapman not
complying with his demand, put him in a great
rage, offering him but 600; he said, in a great
passion, if he could not have his demand, he would
make a great fire and burn me and the babe, in the
view of the town, which was named Fort Royal.
The Frenchman bid the Indian make his fire, 'and
I will, ' says he, 'help you, if you think that will do
you more good than 600 livres, ' calling my master
fool, and speaking roughly to him, bid him be gone.
But at the same time the Frenchman was civil to
me; and, for my encouragement, bid me be of good
cheer, for I should be redeemed, and not go back
with them again.

Retiring now with my master for this night, the
next day I was redeemed for six hundred livres;...

I having been about five months amongst the Indians, in about one month after I got amongst the
French, my dear husband, to my unspeakable comfort and joy, came to me, who was now himself
concerned to redeem his children, two of our
daughters being still captives, and only myself and
two little ones redeemed; and, through great difficulty and trouble, he recovered the younger daughter.
But the eldest we could by no means obtain from
their hands, for the squaw, to whom she was given,
had a son whom she intended my daughter should in
time be prevailed with to marry.   The Indians are
very civil towards their captive women, not offering
any incivility by any indecent carriage, (unless they
be more overcome in liquor,) which is commendable
in them, so far. [3]

Captivity of David Boyd

David Boyd, a 13-year-old western Pennsylvania lad
of Scotch-Irish descent, was captured by the Delaware Indians
and adopted into the tribe.   Few narratives of captivity better

illustrate the love which existed between Indian parents and
an adopted white son than this article which is based on
David Boyd's oral account of his experiences as recalled by
his grandchildren.

On the 10th of February, 1756, John Boyd went
over to Stewart's for a web of cloth.   After he left
home the mother sent David ... to get some dry
wood. ...   David's brother John, then six years old,
went with him.   David took his hatchet with him
and while cutting the brush heard no sound of approaching footsteps.   John, being a short distance
away, screamed.   David looked up, saw a frightful
being standing beside his brother.   He had heard of
ghosts and thought this must be one.   But there
were several of them and he was not long in doubt.

The big fellow said, 'Ugh, Ugh, ' caught David by
his belt and threw him across his shoulder.   Another Indian did likewise with John, and went off
at a fast trot.   A band of eight Indians had left the
main body and surrounded the settler's little home.
Soon they all came to the rendezvous, bringing the
mother, two sisters, Sallie and Rhoda, both older
than David, and the youngest, a brother two and a
half years old.

The mother being in very delicate health was not
able to travel.   She sat down on a fallen tree.
They took her children from her one at a time, except the youngest.   David looked back after he left
her.   She had her hands raised to Heaven and was
praying 'O God be merciful to my children going
among savages. '   He said that prayer was ever
present with him.   He never spoke of it that he did
not shed tears.

As soon as they got the children away the Indians
killed her and the little boy and scalped them.   Two
savages were deputed to do this deed and when they
rejoined the party, with a refinement of cruelty
which it is hard to realize, they gave the scalps to
Sallie and David and forced them to carry them....

By the time the Indians reached their villages the
children were almost naked, having neither clothing
nor shoes.   They made no pause even to take food,

they ate as they ran.   The evening of the third day
they stopped, built a fire, toasted a little bear's
meat which they offered the children while the Indians enjoyed the cheese and other things they had
stolen.   David had no appetite for bear meat and
did not take any.   He was planning to escape from
them that night, but he was secured between two
Indians and the children were not allowed to speak
together.   John cried a great deal; he was too
young to know his danger.   The next morning they
rose very early.   While preparing to start, the old
Indian by whom David was afterward adopted, took
a sharp stick, put a piece of meat on it, held it in
the fire a few moments, pushed the piece back, put
on another, and did likewise till he filled the stick,
and then handed it to David secretly.   David ate
the cooked edges as he ran along, for he had to
run to keep pace with them.   This was the beginning of a long series of kindnesses on the part of
the old chief during the captivity.

When the Indian village in Ohio was reached the
children were separated and the booty that they had
taken during the raid was divided.   David saw them
counting the money his father had taken with him
that morning to the weaver's, consisting of silver
dollars, some of which were cut in halves and
quarters to make change.   By this time he knew
the Stewarts had been killed.   He supposed for a
long time that his father had been killed too, but
the old chief, after the adoption, said they missed
him on the way between the two houses.

The raiding party belonged to the great division of
Indians known as the Iroquois. . . .   David was
claimed by the Delawares, the sisters and younger
brother by some of the other tribes.   Of John no
further account was ever known.   Being young he
may have succumbed to the hardships of barbarous
life, or possibly adopting their customs and habits
he may have lived and died an Indian.

The next year, 1757, David met his sister Sallie
with a party of Indians but he was not allowed to
speak to her.   He never saw his sisters again until they came home in 1763.   They were held prisoners seven years and were exchanged at Detroit. . . .

David was now subjected to a discipline by which
his captors intended to develop a great brave or
have a fit subject for their amusement. For some
time he had to run the gauntlet, which amusement,
for the Indians, consisted in running a prescribed
limit between two lines made up of vindictive squaws
and young savage rogues armed with sticks, stones,
or whatever suited their purpose best, each desirous of touching up the pale-face boy.

This was very degrading to David both mentally and
physically. He set his wits to work to devise some
plan to put a stop to it. The old Chief who had be-
friended him before told him secretly that if he
would catch one of the boys separately where he
would have at least an even chance, and succeed in
giving him a sound thrashing the ceremony would be
dispensed with in the future. He determined to try
the experiment. There was one boy who was particularly ingenious in the cruelties he bestowed, and
David thought if he died in the attempt he would feel
some satisfaction if he could repay this rascal a
little of what he owed him. It was nothing but death
anyway in a short time. Every morning when he
awoke he thought they would kill him that day; every
change he noticed in their countenance he thought
betokened some determination to torture him. Life
under such circumstances one would think would
have but little charm, but to the boy of fourteen
'Hope springs eternal.'

About this time a large party of them went to gather
haws. . . . While they were in the woods at this time
this Indian boy was very insolent to David, and he
thought now or never was his time to avenge himself. He sprang upon his tormentor; they had a
rough and tumble wrestle, but at last the pale-face
found himself on top and he redressed his wrongs
as only an infuriated boy could. Finally a noise
attracted his attention and looking up he saw squaws
and braves running towards him, tomahawks up-
lifted. It was sure death now and as it was his
last chance he redoubled his licks. Coming nearer
and seeing his determination they dropped their
weapons and patted him on the back saying, 'Make
fine Indian, make fine Indian.' This was the turning point with him. His dusky playmates had at

last a wholesome regard for him and he was no
longer a target for every squaw's vengeance.   He
was emancipated from the gauntlet performance.

The first year of his captivity was drawing to a
close.   He still belonged to the tribes in common,
to go and come as he was ordered by any one who
chose to command him. It had been a dreadful year
for him.   He suffered greatly from want of clothing
and great exposure.

It was towards the last of January 1757, when he
missed his old friend from the camp and was
greatly troubled on account of his absence.   He had
felt for some time a sense of protection when he
was near.

When the chief had been absent about two weeks
one morning two warriors came to him tricked out
in all the finery and paint of the war path.   Commanding him to follow them, they took him about
two miles to a river, there they stripped him of
what few tatters he had on and dipped him three
times into the water, each time saying, 'Go down
white man, come up red man. '   Then they shaved
his head, leaving a tuft of hair on the crown,
painted him in the most approved style, put a hunting shirt on him, gave him moccasins, and fastened
the same belt on him that he had on when captured.

They then led him to a pool of water to look at
himself in nature's mirror; the two jumping and
dancing around him seemed delighted with their
handiwork.   David was horrified with his appearance.   He looked so much like an Indian that he
thought he must really be one, and that that was
the way they were made.

They next took him back to the village.   It was all
in commotion.   The warriors were dressed in war
costume, painted and ... ready for marching.   He
was put in front and ... traveled about six miles
in close file until they reached an open space or
natural meadow.   There was a great gathering of
the tribe formed into a large circle.   When the
procession came up the circle opened and he was
ushered in.   There he saw standing in the center

an old brave, all alone, with a large knife in his
hand, looking very stern. He was a stranger to
David and must certainly be the executioner. The
old man advanced, knife in hand, inserted it under
the boy's belt and cut it in twain.

The imagination plays wonderful tricks with us.
David was sure he had received his death blow; he
felt the warm blood trickling to his feet and expected to see it on the ground. At that instant the
chief took him in his arms exclaiming in the Indian
language, 'My son, my son, my son.' David then
recognized his old friend, who made an oration to
the assemblage saying that he called them to witness
that he took this boy to be his son in place of the
one he had lost when on the war trail. After this
he took the belt that he cut off, divided it into many
pieces, giving the largest to his nearest friend. He
gave David an Indian name and presented him with
the hatchet with which the boy was cutting brush
when he was captured.

This was followed by great feasting and dancing,
with plenty of fire water. When they were all en-
gaged in their pastime the old chief quietly with-
drew, and taking his new son sought his own wigwam for he feared that in the drunken carousal
some accident might befall the new made Indian.
The old wife welcomed and claimed him for her
own, bathed his feet, removed the thorns, applied
a healing salve and made life seem worth having
again. Thus even in savage life a woman's kind
offices makes existence endurable.

From this time on he could make no complaint of
his treatment. He shared the good and evil times
of his surroundings. His father was a man of influence in his tribe and his son enjoyed the advantages of his position. The Chief took him to
his heart. . . .

As time passed along David began to be pleased
with his mode of life and became reconciled to his
fate. He never expected to get home. At that age
any boy would be pleased with the desultory life,
rambling over the country, hunting and fishing, en-
gaging in the pastimes of a warlike people.

After several years the old Chief began to feel remorse for having stolen the boy and began to make plans to
return him to his white relatives.   He even sent word of his
intentions to David's father but the elder Boyd refused to believe it.

> The winter had been spent in trapping for furs and
> they had been very successful.   The furs had been
> carefully stored, no sale being made at the usual
> time.   With the taciturnity of his race the chief
> made no explanation of his plans to David, but it
> began to be evident to him that the old man was
> much agitated.
>
> One evening they were sitting in their wigwam--it
> was a little apart from the village--the sun was
> about setting.   He called David's attention to it,
> 'Do you see how swiftly the sun is going down, and
> my sun will soon be set too.   Then I will be in the
> happy hunting grounds where my son is, and I want
> to restore you to your own father before I go. ' ...
> he wanted as far as in him lay, to atone for the
> great wrong that had been done.   He was the very
> Indian that had snatched him from his family and
> left his father childless and homeless.   But he had
> great misgivings about venturing on the journey on
> account of the hostility of the whites; the time had
> been too short to allay the enmity between the
> races.   He would ask David how he thought his
> father would treat him when he would return his
> long lost son to him, then walk back and forth look-
> ing very sad.   He was deeply attached to the son of
> his adoption, but he felt that the red man's fortune
> was waning and he was anxious for the future of the
> boy.   According to his light I know of no nobler
> impulses than had this child of nature.
>
> The old wife was dead and with no near kindred the
> declining years were bearing heavily on the old man.
> David felt loath to leave him to his empty wigwam.
> As the spring opened up the old man made his pre-
> parations slowly but steadily; selecting the best of
> the ponies he packed them with the furs, and they
> started on their eventful journey homewards, in
> different plight than when he made that forced trip
> in the gloomy winter of 1756.   The foster father
> said he would see to their safety through the Indian

territory, but must look to David when they got
among the palefaces. They traveled under a flag
of truce, a white cloth tied to a stick being borne
aloft throughout the journey. It was dangerous yet
for an Indian to be traveling with a white boy in the
colony of Pennsylvania.

They traveled without incident until they reached
Carlisle, arriving in the afternoon. It was soon
noised through the village that an Indian had brought
in a white boy. Thomas Urie, who was soon on the
spot, anxious to see if it were possible he might be
one of his murdered sister's family, made a furious
attack on the old man. Cooler heads intervened; he
was prevented from wrecking his fury on the creature standing under his flag of truce. It was a
bitter pang to Urie that this of all Indians should
go unpunished.

The saddened Chief, in his own dialect, bid David
beware of such a man; he might not be a relative
at all, but David recognized his uncle. Refusing to
hold any parley with an Indian except at the muzzle
of his rifle, he took his nephew out to his own
home. The foster father felt that it was cruel return for all his kindness.

When David recounted to his uncle his history,
dwelling on the noble traits and unvarying kindness
of his friend, the uncle grew more reasonable and
consented to David's return the next morning to the
old Indian.

David was anxious to present his benefactor to his
own father, but Urie refused to allow the Indian to
proceed any farther, saying he could trust no red-
skin out of his sight. This was a great disappointment, as it was the Indian's great desire to take
the boy to his own father's door. Finding the feeling so hostile the old man set about carrying out
the rest of his plan. He sold the furs and ponies
for a considerable sum, bought clothing for the boy
so that he should be presentable and gave all the
rest of the money to David....

It was about twenty miles from Carlisle to Shippensburg. His father lived on the farm whence

David was taken. Things were greatly changed; his
father had remarried; neither mother, sister nor
brother was there to greet him. He had grown
fond of the wild and free life of the forest and was
greatly dissatisfied by his new surroundings. He
determined to rejoin his Indian father and live and
die among the people of his adoption. He had to
be closely guarded for weeks before he relinquished
his plan. He was seventeen years old when he
came back to civilized life. [4]

Captivity of Barbara Leininger

Barbara Leininger was the twelve-year-old sister of
Regina, the "German captive," whose experiences were described in an earlier chapter. Along with a twelve-year-old
girl friend, Marie le Roy, she was captured at Penn's Creek,
Pennsylvania on October 16, 1755, and taken to the Indian
town of Kittanny. After four years of captivity they escaped
and published an account of their adventures which is one of
the best illustrations available of female captives' willingness
to risk death by excruciating torture in order to escape:

Two of the Indians now went to the house of Barbara
Leininger, where they found her father, her brother,
and her sister Regina. Her mother had gone to the
mill. They demanded rum; but there was none in
the house. Then they called for tobacco, which
was given them. Having filled and smoked a pipe,
they said: 'We are Allegheny Indians, and your
cnemics. You must all die!' Thereupon they shot
her father, tomahawked her brother, who was
twenty years of age, took Barbara and her sister
Regina prisoners, and conveyed them into the forest
for about a mile. There they were soon joined by
the other Indians, with Marie le Roy and the little
girl.

Not long after several of the Indians led the prisoners to the top of a high hill, near the two plantations. Toward evening the rest of the savages returned with six fresh and bloody scalps, which they
threw at the feet of the poor captives, saying that
they had a good hunt that day.

The next morning we were taken about two miles

further into the forest, while the most of the Indians again went out to kill and plunder. Toward
evening they returned with nine scalps and five
prisoners.

On the third day the whole band came together and
divided the spoils. In addition to large quantities
of provisions, they had taken fourteen horses and
ten prisoners, namely, one man, one woman, five
girls and three boys. We two girls, as also two
of the horses, fell to the share of an Indian named
Galasko.

We traveled with our new master for two days. He
was tolerably kind, and allowed us to ride all the
way, while he and the rest of the Indians walked.
Of this circumstance Barbara Leininger took advantage and tried to escape. But she was almost
immediately recaptured, and condemned to be
burned alive. The savages gave her a French
Bible, which they had taken from le Roy's house,
in order that she might prepare for death; and,
when she told them that she could not understand
it, they gave her a German Bible. Thereupon they
made a large pile of wood and set it on fire, in-
tending to put her into the midst of it. But a young
Indian begged so earnestly for her life that she was
pardoned, after having promised not to attempt to
escape again, and to stop her crying.

The next day the whole troop was divided into two
bands, the one marching in the direction of the
Ohio, the other, in which we were with Galasko, to
Jenkiklamuhs, a Delaware town on the west branch
of the Susquehanna. There we staid ten days, and
then proceeded to Puncksotonay, or Eschentowb.
Marie le Roy's brother was forced to remain at
Jenkiklamuhs.

After having rested for five days at Puncksotonay,
we took our way to Kittanny. As this was to be
the place of our permanent abode, we here received
our welcome, according to Indian custom. It consisted of three blows each, on the back. There
were, however, administered with great mercy.
Indeed, we concluded that we were beaten merely
in order to keep up an ancient usage, and not with

the intention of injuring us.   The month of December was the time of our arrival, and we remained at Kittanny until the month of September, 1756.

The Indians gave us enough to do.   We had to tan leather, to make shoes (moccasins), to clear land, to plant corn, to cut down trees and build huts, to wash and cook.   The want of provisions, however, caused us the greatest sufferings.   During all the time that we were at Kittanny we had neither lard nor salt; and sometimes we were forced to live on acorns, roots, grass and bark.   There was nothing in the world to make this new sort of food palatable excepting hunger itself.

In the month of September Col. Armstrong arrived with his men and attacked Kittanny Town.   Both of us happened to be in that part of it which lies on the other (right) side of the river (Alleghany).   We were immediately conveyed ten miles farther into the interior, in order that we might have no chance of trying, on this occasion, to escape.   The savages threatened to kill us.   If the English had advanced, this might have happened.   For, at that time, the Indians were greatly in dread of Col. Armstrong's corps.   After the English had withdrawn, we were again brought back to Kittanny, which town had been burned to the ground.

There we had the mournful opportunity of witnessing the cruel end of an English woman, who had attempted to flee out of her captivity and to return to the settlements with Col. Armstrong.   Having been recaptured by the savages, and brought back to Kittanny, she was put to death in an unheard-of way.   First, they scalped her; next, they laid burning splinters of wood, here and there, upon her body; and then they cut off her ears and fingers, forcing them into her mouth so that she had to swallow them.   Amidst such torments, this woman lived from nine o'clock in the morning until toward sunset when a French officer took compassion on her, and put her out of her misery.   An English soldier, on the contrary, named John _____, who escaped from prison at Lancaster, and joined the French, had a piece of flesh cut from her body and ate it.   When she was dead, the Indians chopped her

in two, through the middle, and let her be until the
dogs came and devoured her.

Three days later an Englishman was brought in who
had likewise attempted to escape with Col. Armstrong, and burned alive in the same village. His
torments, however, continued about three hours,
but his screams were frightful to listen to. It
rained that day very hard, so that the Indians could
not keep up the fire. Hence they began to discharge
gunpowder at his body. At last, amidst his worst
pains, when the poor man called for a drink of
water, they brought him melted lead, and poured it
down his throat. This draught at once helped him
out of the hands of the barbarians, for he died on
the instant.

It is easy to imagine what an impression such fearful instances of cruelty make upon the mind of a
poor captive. Does he attempt to escape from the
savages, he knows in advance that, if retaken, he
will be roasted alive. Hence he must compare two
evils, namely, either to remain among them a
prisoner forever, or to die a cruel death. Is he
fully resolved to endure the latter, then he may run
away with a brave heart.

Soon after these occurrences we were brought to
Fort Duquesne, where we remained for about two
months. We worked for the French, and our Indian master drew our wages. In this place, thank
God, we could again eat bread. Half a pound was
given us daily. We might have had bacon, too, but
we took none of it, for it was not good. In some
respects we were better off than in the Indian
towns; we could not, however, abide the French.
They tried hard to induce us to forsake the Indians
and stay with them, making us various favorable
offers. But we believed that it would be better for
us to remain among the Indians, inasmuch as they
would be more likely to make peace with the English than the French, and inasmuch as there would
be more ways open for flight in the forest than in
a fort. Consequently we declined the offers of the
French and accompanied our Indian master to
Sackum, where we spent the winter, keeping house
for the savages, who were continually on the chase.

In the spring we were taken to Kaschkaschking, an
Indian town on the Beaver Creek.   There we again
had to clear the plantations of the Indian nobles,
after the German fashion, to plant corn, and to do
other hard work of every kind.   We remained at
this place for about a year and a half.

After having, in the past three years, seen no one
of our own flesh and blood, except those unhappy
beings who, like ourselves, were bearing the yoke
of the heaviest slavery, we had the unexpected
pleasure of meeting with a German, who was not a
captive, but free, and who, as we heard, had been
sent into this neighborhood to negotiate a peace between the English and the natives.   His name was
Frederick Post.   We and all the other prisoners
heartily wished him success and God's blessing upon
his undertaking.   We were, however, not allowed
to speak with him.   The Indians gave us plainly to
understand that any attempt to do this would be
taken amiss.   He himself, by the reserve with which
he treated us, let us see that this was not the time
to talk over our affictions.   But we were greatly
alarmed on his account.   For the French told us
that, if they caught him, they would roast him alive
for five days, and many Indians declared that it was
impossible for him to get safely through, that he
was destined for death.

Last summer the French and Indians were defeated
by the English in a battle fought at Loyal-Hannon,
or Fort Ligonier.   This caused the utmost conster-
nation among the natives.   They brought their wives
and children from Lockstown, Sackum, Schomingo,
Mamalty, Kaschkaschkung, and other places in that
neighborhood, to Moschkingo, about one hundred
and fifty miles farther west.   Before leaving, however, they destroyed their crops, and burned
everything which they could not carry with them.
We had to go along, and staid at Moschkingo the
whole winter.

In February Barbara Leininger agreed with an Englishman named David Breckenreach (Breckenridge),
to escape, and gave her comrade, Marie le Roy,
notice of their intentions.   On account of the severe
season of the year, and the long journey which lay

before them, Marie strongly advised her to re-
linquish the project, suggesting that it should be
postponed until spring, when the weather would be
milder, and promising to accompany her at that
time.

On the last day of February nearly all the Indians
left Moschkingo, and proceeded to Pittsburgh to sell
pelts.   Meanwhile their women traveled ten miles
up the country to gather roots and we accompanied
them.   Two men went along as a guard.   It was our
earnest hope that the opportunity for flight, so long
desired, had now come.   Accordingly, Barbara
Leininger pretended to be sick, so that she might
be allowed to put up a hut for herself alone.   On
the fourteenth of March Marie le Roy was sent back
to the town in order to fetch two young dogs which
had been left there; and, on the same day, Barbara
Leininger came out of her hut and visited a German
woman, ten miles from Moschkingo.   This woman's
name is Mary _____, and she is the wife of a
miller from the South Branch.   She had made every
preparation to accompany us on our flight; but Barbara found that she had in the meanwhile become
lame, and could not think of going along.   She, however, gave Barbara the provisions which she had
stored, namely, two pounds of dried meat, a quart
of corn, and four pounds of sugar.   Besides, she
presented her with pelts for moccasins.   Moreover,
she advised a young Englishman, Owen Gibson, to
flee with us two girls.

On the sixteenth of March, in the evening, Gibson
reached Barbara Leininger's hut, and, at ten
o'clock, our whole party, consisting of us two girls,
Gibson and David Breckenreach, left Moschkingo.
This town lies on a river in the country of the
Dellamottinoes.   We had to pass many huts inhabited
by the savages, and knew that there were at least
sixteen dogs with them.   In the merciful providence
of God not a single one of these dogs barked. Their
barking would at once have betrayed us and frus-
trated our designs.

It is hard to describe the anxious fears of a poor
woman under such circumstances.   The extreme
probability that the Indians would pursue and re-

capture us, was as two to one compared with the
dim hope that, perhaps, we would get through in
safety. But, even if we escaped the Indians, how
would we ever succeed in passing through the wilderness, unacquainted with a single path or trail,
without a guide, and helpless, half naked, broken
down by more than three years of hard slavery,
hungry and scarcely any food, the season wet and
cold, and many rivers and streams to cross? Under such circumstances to depend upon one's own
sagacity would be the worst of follies. If one could
not believe that there is a God, who helps and
saves from death, one had better let running away
alone.

We safely reached the river (Muskingum). ... we
found a raft left by the Indians. Thanking God that
He had himself prepared a way for us across these
first waters, we got on board and pushed off. But
we were carried almost a mile down the river before we could reach the other side. There our
journey began in good earnest. Full of anxiety and
fear, we fairly ran that whole night and all next
day, when we lay down to rest without venturing to
kindle a fire. Early the next morning Owen Gibson
fired at a bear. The animal fell, but, when he ran
with his tomahawk to kill it, it jumped up and bit
him in the feet, leaving three wounds. We all
hastened to his assistance. The bear escaped into
narrow holes among the rocks, where we could not
follow. On the third day, however, Owen Gibson
shot a deer. We cut off the hind quarters and
roasted them at night. The next morning he again
shot a deer, which furnished us with food for that
day. In the evening we got to the Ohio at last,
having made a circuit of over one hundred miles in
order to reach it.

About midnight the two Englishmen rose and began
to work at a raft, which was finished by morning.
We got on board and safely crossed the river. From
the signs which the Indians had there put up we saw
that we were about one hundred and fifty miles from
Fort Duquesne. After a brief consultation we resolved, heedless of path or trail, to travel straight
toward the rising of the sun. This we did for seven
days. On the seventh we found that we had reached

the Little Beaver Creek, and were about fifty miles
from Pittsburgh.

And now, that we imagined ourselves so near the
end of all our troubles and misery, a whole host of
mishaps came upon us. Our provisions were at an
end; Barbara Leininger fell into the water and was
nearly drowned; and, worst misfortune of all, Owen
Gibson lost his flint and steel. Hence we had to
spend four nights without fire, amidst rain and snow.

On the last day of March we came to a river, Alloquepy, about three miles below Pittsburgh. Here
we made a raft, which, however, proved to be too
light to carry us across. It threatened to sink, and
Marie le Roy fell off and narrowly escaped drown-
ing. We had to put back, and let one of our men
convey one of us across at a time. In this way we
reached the Monongalla River, on the other side of
Pittsburgh, the same evening. [5]

Captivity of John M'Cullough

    John M'Cullough was eight years old when captured on
July 26, 1756, near Fort Loudoun, Pennsylvania, by Delaware
Indians. He was adopted by a warrior to replace a brother
who had been killed. After remaining with the Indians several
years he was seen by Andrew Wilkins, a trader, who told
John's father where he was held. Mr. M'Cullough twice entered the Indian country but on neither occasion did he succeed in bringing his son home. Eventually John was recovered by the Bouquet Expedition. After his redemption, John
wrote an account of his captivity which is one of the best
available of the determination of captives to resist return to
their white families:

        The fall following, my white father went out to fort
        Venenggo, or French Creek, along with Wilkins.
        Wilkins sent a special messenger to Mohoning, for
        my Indian brother to take me to Venenggo, telling
        him that my father would purchase me from him;
        accordingly he took me off without letting me know
        his intention, or, it is probable, I would not have
        gone with him; when we got to Venenggo, we en-
        camped about a mile from the garrison; my brother
        went to the garrison to bargain with my father for

me, but told me nothing of it. The next morning
my father and two others came to our camp, and
told me that my brother wanted to see me at the
fort; I must go home with my father, to see my
mother and the rest of my friends; I wept bitterly,
all to no purpose; my father was ready to start;
They laid hold of me and set me on a horse, I
threw myself off; they set me on again, and tied
my legs under the horse's belly, and started away
for Pittsburg[h]; we encamped about ten or fifteen
miles from Venenggo; before we lay down, my
father took his garters and tied my arms behind my
back; however, I had them loose before my father
lay down; I took care to keep it concealed from them
by keeping my arms back as if they were tied.
About midnight, I arose from between my father and
John Simeons, who was to accompany us to Pittsburg; I stepped out from the fire and sat down as
if I had a real necessity for doing so; my father
and Simeons arose and mended up the fire; whilst
they were laying the chunks together--I ran off as
fast as I could. I had got near a hundred yards
from the camp, when I heard them hunting a large
dog, which they had along with them, after me; I
thought the dog would certainly overtake me; I
therefore climbed up a tall tree, as fast as I could;
the dog stopped at the root of the tree, but as they
continued to hunt him on, he ran off again--they
came past the tree; after they passed by me, I
climbed further up, until I got to some limbs, where
I could rest myself; the dog came back to the tree
again--after a short time they came back and stood
a considerable time at the root of the tree--then
returned to the fire; I could see them distinctly
from where I was; I remained on the tree about an
hour; I then went down and steered through the
woods till I found the road; I went about two or
three miles along it, and the wolves were making
a hideous noise all around me: I went off the road
a short distance and climbed up a dogwood sapling,
and fixed myself on the branches of it, where I remained till break of day; I then got on the road
again; I ran along as fast as I was able, for about
five miles, where I came to an Indian camp: they
told me that I had better not keep the road, alledg-
ing that I would certainly be pursued; I took their
advice and went off the road immediately, and

steered through the woods till I got to where my
friends were encamped, they advised me to take
along the road that we came, when we came there,
telling me that they were going to return home that
day; I made no delay, but went on about ten miles,
and there waited till they came up with me. Not
long after I left them, my father came to the camp;
They denied that they had seen me--supposing that
I had gone on to Mohoning by myself, telling him
that if I had, that they would take me to Pittsburg
that fall.

Soon after we got home to Mohoning, instead of
taking me to Pittsburg, agreeable to their promise,
they set out on their fall hunt, taking me along with
them; we staid out till some time in the winter before we returned.

John remained with the Indians two more years. The
Delawares were hostile to white people and he witnessed the
murder of a number of traders but did not take part in any
raids. After Col. Bouquet invaded the Indian country John
was among the first of the captives surrendered under the
terms he imposed upon them. He had been held eight years
and four months. [6]

Notes

1. Robert F. Spencer and Jesse D. Jennings, The Native
   Americans. (New York, 1965), 1-5.

2. Garcilaso de la Vega, The Florida of the Inca. (Austin,
   1951), 63-79.

3. Elizabeth Hanson, God's Mercy Surmounting Man's
   Cruelty, in Samuel G. Drake, Tragedies of the Wilderness. (Boston, 1846), 114-26.

4. Mrs. Elvert M. Davis, "History of the Capture and Captivity of David Boyd from Cumberland County Pennsylvania, 1756, " in Western Pennsylvania Historical
   Magazine, XIV (1931), 28-39.

5. Leininger and le Roy, "Narrative, " 112-22.

6. John M'Cullough, A Narrative of the Captivity of John
   M'Cullough, in Loudon, Selection of Some of the Most Interesting Narratives, I, 252-301.

Chapter 6

TREATMENT OF CAPTIVES
WEST OF THE MISSISSIPPI

John Hunter was captured about 1801, probably in
Missouri. He was so young that he retained no memory of
his white family. He never knew his real name but he became so adept at killing game with a bow and arrow that the
Indians called him "Hunter" and he retained the name.

After living with the Indians many years, Hunter had
to leave them when he warned a party of white men of an
impending massacre. His narrative is a long and interesting
one. Only a few passages which illustrate the course of assimilation can be presented here.

> I was taken prisoner at a very early period of my
> life by a party of Indians, who, from the train of
> events that followed, belonged to, or were in alli-
> ance with the Kickapoo nation. At the same time,
> two other white children, a boy and a small girl,
> were also made prisoners.

> I have too imperfect a recollection of the circum-
> stances connected with this capture, to attempt any
> account of them, although I have reflected on the
> subject so often, and with so great interest and in-
> tensity, under the knowledge I have since acquired
> of the Indian modes of warfare, as nearly to es-
> tablish at times a conviction in my mind of a per-
> fect rememberance. In these deluded spells I see
> the rush of the Indians, hear their war whoops and
> terrific yells, and witness the massacre of my
> parents and connections, the pillage of their pro-
> perty, and the incendious destruction of their dwell-
> ings. But the first incident that made an actual
> and prominent impression on me, happened while
> the party were somewhere encamped, no doubt
> shortly after my capture: it was as follows: The
> little girl whom I before mentioned, beginning to

75

cry, was immediately despatched with the blow of a
tomahawk from one of the warriors: the circumstance terrified me very much, more particularly
as it was followed with very menacing motions of
the same instrument, directed to me, and then
pointed to the slaughtered infant, by the same warrior, which I then interpreted to signify, that if I
cried, he would serve me in the same manner.
From this period till the apprehension of personal
danger had subsided, I recollect many of the occurrences which took place.

Soon after the above transaction, we proceeded on
our journey till a party separated from the main
body, and took the boy before noticed with them,
which was the last I saw or heard of him.

The Indians generally separate their white prisoners.   The practice no doubt originated more with
a view to hasten a reconciliation to their change,
and a nationalization of feelings, than with any intention of wanton cruelty.

The Indians who retained me continued their march,
chiefly through woods, for several successive days;
a circumstance well remembered by me, because
the fear of being left behind called forth all my
efforts to keep up with them, whenever from fatigue
or any other cause they compelled me to walk,
which was often the case.

After a long march and much fatigue, we reached
their camps, which were situated on a considerable
stream of water, but in what particular part or
section of country, I am wholly unable to say. Just
before our arrival, however, we were met by a
great number of old men, women, and children,
among whom was a white woman attired in the Indian costume; she was the wife of a principal chief,
was a great friend to the Indians, and joined with,
and I believe surpassed the squaws in the extrava-
gancy of her exultations and rejoicings on account
of the safe return of the warriors with prisoners,
scalps, and other trophies....

As I grew larger so as to recollect the more recent incidents of my life, the Indian boys were ac-

customed tauntingly to upbraid me with being white,
and with the whites all being squaws. ...

The white woman whom I noticed a little back, was
no way remarkable for any attention to me, which
at this period of my life I think somewhat extra-
ordinary; but perhaps, like myself, she had been
taken prisoner by the Indians while young, and her
sympathies had become enlisted for, or identified
with those of the tribe.   She had two children, was
tall, healthy, and good-looking. ...

Digressing a little, I may here observe that I met
three or four white children, apparently of my own
age, while travelling among the different tribes.
They appeared like myself to have been at first
forced to assume the Indian character and habits;
but time, and a conformity to custom had nation-
alized them, and they seemed as happy and contented as though they had descended directly from
the Indians, and were in possession of their patri-
mony.   I also met some, whose parents, either on
the side of the father or mother, had been white;
they sustained the character of brave warriors; but
in general no cast, differing from that of the tribe,
is held in repute or estimation.   It is a remarkable fact, that white people generally when brought
up among the Indians, become unalterably attached
to their customs, and seldom afterwards abandon
them.   I have known two instances of white persons, who had arrived at manhood, leaving their
connections, and civilized habits, assuming the Indian, and fulfilling all his duties.   These, however,
happened among the Cherokees.   Thus far I am an
exception. ...

Hunter was treated brutally by the Kickapoos during a
captivity which lasted several years.   Then during the course
of tribal warfare he was captured by the Kansas Indians.
Shortly after his arrival in their village he was adopted by a
family to replace a son who had been killed by the Pawnees.
His adopted mother treated him with great kindness and when
she died he sincerely mourned her loss.

The squaw who had adopted me among her children,
and who had treated me with great tenderness and
affection, was accidentally drowned in attempting to

collect drift wood, during the prevalence of a flood.
This circumstance was the cause of grief, apparently
more poignant to be endured than is usually experienced in civilized life; because, the customs of the
Indians do not tolerate the same open expression of
feelings, from the indulgence of which the acuteness
of grief is relieved, and sooner subsides.   The Indians regard tears; or any expression of grief, as
a mark of weakness in males, and unworthy of the
character of the warrior.   In obedience to this custom, I bore my affliction in silence, in order to
sustain my claims to their respect and esteem; but
nevertheless, I sincerely and deeply felt the bereavement; and cannot even at this late day, reflect
on her maternal conduct to me, from the time I was
taken prisoner by the Kansas, to her death, without
the association of feelings, to which, in other respects I am a stranger.   She was indeed a mother
to me; and I feel my bosom dilate with gratitude at
the recollection of her goodness, and care of me
during this helpless period of my life.   This, to
those who have been bred in refinement and ease,
under the fond and watchful guardianship of parents,
may appear gross and incongruous.   If, however,
the imagination be allowed scope, and a lad ten or
twelve years of age, without kindred or name, or
any knowledge by which he could arrive at an acquaintance with any of the circumstances connected
with his being, be supposed in the central wilds of
North America, nearly a thousand miles from any
white settlement, a prisoner or sojourner among a
people, on whom he had not the slightest claim, and
with whose language, habits and character, he was
wholly unacquainted; but, who nevertheless treated
him kindly; and it will appear not only natural but
rational, that he should return such kindness with
gratitude and affection.   Such nearly was my situation, and such in fact were my feelings at that time;
and however my circumstances have since changed,
or however they may change in the future, I have
no hope of seeing happier days than I experienced
at this early period of my life, while sojourning
with the Kansas nation, on the Kansas river, some
hundred miles above its confluence with the Missouri. [1]

Captivity of John Rodgers Jewitt

John Jewitt was born in England in 1783. At the age
of 20 he sailed on the ship Boston for China by way of the
Pacific Coast of North America. On March 12, 1803, the
ship arrived at Nootka Sound to trade trinkets to the Indians
for furs which would be exchanged for valuable goods in
China. The captain insulted Chief Maquina of the Nootka
tribe and the Indians seized the ship and beheaded every man
on board except Jewitt (an armorer) and one Thompson (a
sailmaker) whose skills could be used. The chief protected
them from the warriors who wanted to kill them. He became
fond of John and treated him well. John eventually became
an adopted member of the tribe and a slave-owner, as was
the custom among the Indians of the Northwest Coast. Finally, after two years with the Nootkas, he and Thompson
were rescued by a passing ship.

John kept a journal during his captivity. Only a brief
excerpt from this unique story can be presented here.

> In July Maquina informed me that he was going to
> war with the Aytcharts, a tribe about fifty miles to
> the south, and that I must make daggers for his
> men. . . .
>
> The Aytcharts, taken by surprise, were unable to
> resist. Except for a few who escaped, all were
> killed or taken prisoner. I had the good fortune to
> take four captives. Maquina, as a favor, permitted
> me to consider them as mine, and occasionally em-
> ploy them in fishing for me. Thompson, who
> thirsted for revenge, succeeded in killing seven
> stout fellows, an act which won him the admiration
> of Maquina and the chiefs.
>
> After putting to death all the old and infirm of
> either sex and destroying the buildings, we re-em-
> barked for Nootka with our booty. We were re-
> ceived with great joy by the women and children,
> accompanying our war song with a most furious
> drumming on the houses. The next day a great
> feast was given by Maquina in celebration of his
> victory. . . .
>
> Soon after we reached Tashees, Maquina informed
> me that he and his chiefs had determined I must

marry one of their women. He said the sooner I
adopted their customs the better, and that a wife
and family would make me more contented with
their mode of living. I objected strongly, but he
told me that, should I refuse, both Thompson and
myself would be put to death. He added, however,
that if none of the women of his tribe pleased me,
he would go with me to some of the other tribes,
where he would purchase for me any woman I
should select. With death on the one side and ma-
trimony on the other, I thought proper to choose
the lesser of the two evils. As I did not fancy any
of the Nootka women, I asked to be permitted to
make choice of one from some other tribe.

The next morning Maquina, with about fifty men in
two canoes, set out with me for Aitizzart, taking a
quantity of cloth, muskets, sea-otter skins, etc.,
for the purchase of my bride. With the aid of our
paddles and sails we arrived at the village before
sunset. Our arrival excited a general alarm; the
men hastened to the shore, armed with weapons,
and made many warlike gestures. We remained
quietly in our canoes. Finally the messenger of
the chief came to invite us on shore. We followed
him to the chief's house, where we were ushered
in with much ceremony. My seat was next to
Maquina. . . .

After a feast of herring spawn and oil, Maquina
asked me if I saw any that I liked among the women there. I immediately pointed out a girl of
about seventeen, the daughter of Upquesta, the
chief. . . . the chief gave me his daughter, with
an earnest request that I would use her well, which
I promised him. She accompanied me with apparent satisfaction on board the canoe.

When we reached Tashees all the inhabitants were
collected on the shore and welcomed us with loud
shouts. The women conducted my bride to Maquina's house and kept her with them for ten days.
It was the custom that no intercourse should take
place between the newly married pair during that
period. At night Maquina gave a great feast, followed by a dance in which all the women joined,
and thus ended the festivities. . . .

I found my Indian princess both amiable and intel-
ligent. She was very attentive to keeping her
garments and person neat and clean, and appeared
eager to please me. She was, I have said, about
seventeen. Her person was small but well formed,
as were her features. Her complexion was fairer
than any of the women, with considerable color in
her cheeks, her hair long, black, and much softer
than is usual with them, and her teeth small, even,
and a dazzling whiteness. Her expression indicated
sweetness of temper and modesty. She would indeed have been considered very pretty in any
country.

With a partner possessing so many attractions,
many may conclude that I must have found myself
comparatively happy. But a compulsory marriage,
even with the most beautiful and accomplished person in the world, can never prove a source of real
happiness. I could not but view my marriage as a
chain that was to bind me down to this savage land.
In a few days Maquina informed me there had been
a meeting of his chiefs and it had been determined
that, as I had married one of their women, I must
be considered one of them and conform to their
customs. In future, neither myself nor Thompson
was to wear our European clothes, but dress in
kutsaks or mantles like themselves. This order
was most painful to me.

... I suppose I fell sick because I had suffered so
much from the cold, in going without proper clothing. For a number of hours I was in great pain
and expected to die. When the fever left me, I
was so weak as scarcely to be able to stand. I
had nothing comforting to take, nor anything to
drink but cold water.

My Indian wife, as far as she knew how, did everything for me she could. But the feebleness in
which my disorder had left me, the dejection I felt
at the almost hopelessness of my situation and the
want of warm clothing and civilized nursing still
kept me very much indisposed. Maquina perceived
this. He finally told me that if I did not like living
with my wife, and that was the cause of my being
so sad, I might part with her. I readily accepted

this proposal and the next day Maquina sent her
back to her father.

On parting with me she showed much emotion. She
begged me to allow her to remain till I had recovered, as there was no one who would take such
good care of me as herself. But I told her she
must go, as I honestly did not think I should ever
get well. She took an affectionate leave, and left
her two slaves to take care of me.

I was greatly affected with the simple expressions
of her regard for me, and could not but feel
strongly concerned for this poor girl. Had it not
been that I considered her a serious obstacle to my
being permitted to leave the country, I should have
felt a real sense of loss. After her departure, I
requested Maquina to permit me to wear warmer
clothing or I should certainly die from the cold.
He consented, and I was once more comfortably
clad. In a short time the change of clothing restored me to health, and I again went to work making harpoons for Maquina. [2]

Captivity of Mrs. Sarah Ann Horn

Mrs. Sarah Ann Horn was born in Huntington, England, in 1809. In 1835 she, with her husband and two small
children, joined the colony of Dr. John C. Beals on Las
Moras Creek, near its juncture with the Rio Grande, in
Southwestern Texas. The colonists were chiefly from New
York, England and Germany. There were no experienced
frontiersmen among them and when the Texas Revolution broke
out the people abandoned the settlement and fled in small
groups.

The Horn and Harris families were in a party which
attempted to reach safety at Matamoros, Mexico. They fell
into the hands of the Comanches on April 4, 1836, and Mrs.
Horn remained in captivity for more than a year. Finally
she was redeemed by a trader. She wrote an account of her
experiences in an attempt to obtain funds to help rescue her
lost children. Like most women who were taken by Plains
Indians, she suffered too many ordeals to long survive after
her redemption. "... soon my hopes and fears shall be
hushed in death, " she concluded her story, and soon she died.

A few passages from her long and interesting narrative follow:

> Before they laid down for the night, Mrs. Harris
> and myself were bound by passing a cord about our
> ancles and arms, so as to bring them close to our
> sides. ... the whole of that dreadful night, my
> agonized heart seemed ready to burst, as I listened
> to the cries of my orphan babes, as they called for
> their murdered father, and for water to quench
> their thirst....

> There was one Indian woman among them, who be-
> longed to the party that claimed Mrs. Harris for
> their prisoner;--she was very small in her person,
> and I should think not more than twenty years of
> age; but of all the depraved beings I have seen ...
> I think she excelled. I have often seen her take
> her by the throat and choke her, until the poor un-
> resisting creature would turn black in the face, and
> fall as if dead at her feet; and then, to finish the
> tragedy, her cruel master would jump on her with
> his feet, and stamp her, until I have thought her
> sufferings were at an end.

After killing a number of ranchers near Matamoros,
the Indians, fearing pursuit, moved northward at a rapid
pace. The prisoners were tied to the back of mules and
seldom permitted to eat or drink.

> During the whole of this long and painful journey ...
> much of our way was over rough, stony ground,
> frequently cut up by steep and dangerous fords. At
> one of these last, with high and rugged banks, my
> little Joseph slipped off the mule into the water, as
> the creature was struggling to ascend the uneven
> bank. The boy behind whom he rode was cross,
> and would not suffer him to hold on by him. I had
> just gained the shore, and turning around saw the
> child in his endeavors to extricate himself from his
> perilous situation. He had nearly succeeded, when
> one of the savages, enraged at the accident, stabbed
> the little creature in the face with his lance, and
> sent him back into the midst of the foaming stream.
> The wound was inflicted just below the eye, and
> was a very severe one ... but the poor suffering
> little creature made another effort, and, with the
> blood streaming down his naked body from his

wounded face, gained the shore. On this occasion
the feelings of the mother triumphed over ever
other consideration, and I upbraided the wretch for
his cruelty. But bitterly did he make me pay for
my temerity.... When we halted for the night,
the savage, seated on his mule, called me to him.
As I approached him in obedience to his lordly
command, he held his whip in one hand, and drew
his knife with the other. But the deadly steel had
no terrors for a miserable wretch like me; I felt
that the bitterness of death was past. With his
whip he gave me many cruel stripes; but so much
keener was the anguish of my soul, than any that
even a savage could inflict upon my almost naked
body, that his strokes seemed to me of no more
weight than a feather. ... my soul ... would fain
have preferred the most cruel death to life such as
mine.

A number of the Indians then took my children and
returned with them to the stream we had just passed. They were absent about an hour, when I saw
them at a distance returning, holding the children
up by their hands; and I observed that when they let
go of them, which they did several times, they fell
as though they were dead. On their arrival at the
camp, they were a sight to behold! Their emaci-
ated bodies were enormously distended, and Joseph's
face, from the wound he had received, was dread-
fully swollen. They were quite insensible for some
time, and the water was discharging continually
from their mouth, nose, and ears. The Indians, it
appeared, had been amusing themselves by throwing
them into the stream, and when nearly drowned
would take them out. John was a little more than
five, and Joseph less than four years old.

The Indians moved on into New Mexico and Mrs.
Horn's children were taken from her and adopted by families
in other bands. Some white traders attempted to redeem the
family but the Indians refused. Joseph's adopted mother was
a Mexican who had been captured as a child and married a
warrior. She treated the child well.

In June, some Mexican Comancheros (traders) tried to
purchase Mrs. Horn but her master would not sell her. They
succeeded in redeeming Mrs. Harris. About three months

later the Comanches camped near San Miguel, New Mexico.
"At this place I was told by an Indian girl, that I was to be
sold to ... the Spaniards, " she wrote.   "I told her ... that
I did not wish to be sold.   Indeed, I felt that the only remaining tie (my dear children) which bound me to this
wretched planet, was among them, and while this was the
case, I infinitely preferred remaining with or near them, to
any condition. "

   After a year and five months of captivity Mrs. Horn
was redeemed by a San Miguel citizen.   An expedition was
sent by traders to try to recover the children.   When they
returned with information that John had frozen to death and
Joseph could not be purchased at any price, Mrs. Horn returned to the United States. [3]

Captivity of Olive Oatman

   Olive Oatman was a 14-year-old Illinois farm girl, the
daughter of Ross Oatman, a Mormon who answered the call
of the Rev. James Brewster to establish a new Zion on the
Colorado River.   The family consisted of the father, mother,
and seven children.   They traveled as part of a large wagon
train as far as Tucson, Arizona, where a dispute caused the
party to break up.   On March 11, 1851, the Oatman family
pushed on alone into the Arizona desert.   On March 18, they
were attacked with warclubs by fierce Tonto raiders.   The
father, mother and four children were killed.   Olive and her
younger sister, Mary, were captured.   Lorenzo, the oldest
boy in the family, was left for dead but finally regained consciousness and was picked up by a wagon train.   He spent
the next five years trying to locate and redeem his sisters.
Finally, with the help of the Army and a Yuma Indian, he
obtained Olive's release. [4]   The story of her captivity was
told to R. B. Stratton.   Her story provides perhaps the best
account of the treatment of female prisoners by Indians of
the Southwestern deserts.

   The Indians took from them their hats and shoes,
   and started on their march.   An Indian led; the two
   captives followed; the other Indians formed the rear-
   guard.   Across the desert they hurried, the tender
   feet of the captives being bruised at every step.
   Sharp stones gashed them, and cactus thorns pierced
   them cruelly.   After several hours Mary sank down
   and refused to go farther.   Blows and threats had

no effect upon her.   She said she had rather die
than live.   At length one of the Indians threw her
across his back, and the march was resumed.
Olive became so faint and weary that she felt she
could not go on, but the fear of being separated
from her sister gave her superhuman energy.

... as they were passing through a dark cañon, a
band of eleven Indians appeared, and approached
them in great excitement.   One of them drew his
bow and let fly an arrow at Olive, which pierced
her dress but did not harm her.   As he fitted another to his bow the captors sprang forward and
placed themselves before the girls, while one of
them seized the would-be assassin.   It appeared
that this man had lost a brother in a recent attack
upon some whites, and had sworn to avenge himself upon the first white that he met.   The captors,
however, had other uses for their captives, and
finally succeeded in getting rid of the avengers,
though not until there had almost been a general
battle.   They travelled until midnight.   In the morning they hurried on till they came to a village of
low, thatched huts.   The captives, suffering and
exhausted by two hundred miles of cruel marching,
were placed on a pile of brush, around which all
the inhabitants of the village, about three hundred
in number, whirled in a dance of exultation and
savage joy.   Throughout it they took every means
of humiliating the captives, by striking them,
throwing dirt upon them, and spitting in their faces.
Their insults had but little effect on the wretched
girls, who had now reached the stage of indiffer-
ence and desperation.   The only apprehension that
troubled them was the fear of torture.   This was
dispelled on the succeeding day.   The jubilee and
feast were over.   A night's rest had somewhat re-
freshed the captives and eased their pains.   They
were set to work at the employments which must
henceforth engage them.   Their fate was now clear.
They were slaves.

It would be difficult to imagine a more oppressive
slavery than that in which they existed.   The Tontos were a people of the most degraded character. ...   Their women were obliged to do all the work,
as in most of the tribes, and, to make their lot

more unenviable, the Tontos had a theory that young
females should not subsist on meat any more than
was absolutely necessary to prevent starvation. In
consequence their women of all ages were dwarfed
and dried up, while their young girls frequently died
from want of food.   To these enslaved and half-
starved squaws the Oatman girls were sub-slaves,
and they found them most cruel mistresses. They
delighted in inventing new and unnecessary tasks,
and at the least provocation beat the helpless
children unmercifully.   The girls quickly learned
that the children of the tribe were their masters,
also, for the slightest complaint from one of these
youngsters was the signal for a severe beating. All
this, and their constant menial labor, had to be un-
dergone on the most stinted allowance of food.
Even in feast times the savages would contemptu-
ously throw them refuse scraps of food, saying:
'You have been fed too well; we will teach you to
live on little. ' They would have died of starvation
if they had not appropriated for themselves, at
every possible occasion, the roots and other food
that they were ordered to gather for their owners.

After about six months of captivity the girls were sold
to the Mohave Indians.   The price was two horses, three
blankets, some vegetables, and beads.   As so frequently happened when moving from one tribe to another the captives
experienced a marked change in treatment.

Another long and weary march was before the girls,
but what they suffered now was not a result of
spite.   The chief's daughter walked all the way,
carrying a roll of blankets that she shared each
night with the captives, while the two horses that
remained to the party were carrying the gentlemen.
For eleven days they trudged along, over rugged
mountains and across dusty deserts, until they
reached the Mohave valley....   Here dwelt the new
owners of the slaves.   As masters they were far
preferable to the Tontos.   They seemed to lack
much of that savage trait of torturing for the pleasure of seeing pain.   They lived in rude but comfortable huts....

To discourage the girls from trying to escape, the
Mohaves tattooed their faces in the manner of women who

are ready for marriage.   Olive asserted, however, that they
were never treated like wives.

        The tribe experienced a famine in 1853 which resulted
in worse treatment of the captives.   Olive was forced to
scour the desert for food for her captors.   If she found any
they seized it immediately,   while Mary, who was too weak
to move about,   received nothing to eat.   Finally Mary starved
to death.

> Oppressed by a terrible feeling of loneliness, Olive
> lived on through the famine.   The next year was
> one of plenty, but it brought her a new torture.
> When the growth of the year had advanced suffici-
> ently to furnish the Mohaves with food, and they
> had recovered strength and spirit, they decided to
> make an expedition against the Cocopahs.   This
> was the first one that they had undertaken since
> the purchase of the captives, and Olive was in-
> formed that in case any of the warriors were
> killed she would be sacrificed, in accordance with
> their custom, which requires a warrior who falls
> in battle to be furnished with a slave. . . .   In des-
> peration she went to the village to learn her fate.
> She sat in silence through the convening and open-
> ing of a council, that Indian decorum made neces-
> sary before the news was told.   At length the mes-
> senger spoke.   The Mohaves were returning in
> triumph with five prisoners.   None of them had
> been killed.

        One of the captive Cocopah women attempted to es-
cape, but she was retaken and crucified.   Olive, compelled
to watch, was warned that a similar fate awaited her if she
tried to run away.   After this she gave up any thought of
escape. [5]

        It is evident from her narrative that by the fifth year
of captivity she was beginning to accept the Indian life despite
its terrors and hardships, but release interrupted the assimilation process.   "To escape seemed impossible, " she wrote,
"and to make an unsuccessful attempt would be worse than
death.   Friends or kindred to look after or care for me, I
had none. . . .   I thought it best to receive my daily allotment
with submission. . . .   Time seemed to make a more rapid
flight; I hardly could wake up to the reality of so long a captivity among savages, and really imagined myself happy for
short periods.

"I considered my age, my sex, my exposure, and was again in trouble, although to the honor of these savages let it be said, that they never offered the least unchaste abuse to me. "[6]

Captivity of Nelson Lee

Nelson Lee was born in 1807. In 1855 he set out with several companions to trail a herd of horses and mules from Texas to California. They were about 350 miles northwest of Eagle Pass, Texas, when the Comanches captured him during a night-time raid on the camp. After three years of captivity he escaped by killing his captor and told his story to a writer who published it.

> Immediately after the council had adjourned, I dis-
> covered the warriors assembling outside the village
> at a point distant a quarter of a mile. At length,
> I was taken by a strong guard and escorted into
> their midst. I found my fellow captives had pre-
> ceded me. There was Aikens, Martin, and Stew-
> art, stripped entirely naked, and bound as follows:
> High posts had been driven in the ground about
> three feet apart. Standing between them, their
> arms had been drawn up as far as they could reach,
> the right hand tied to the stake on the right side
> and the left hand to the stake opposite. Their feet,
> likewise, were tied to the posts near the ground.
>
> Martin and Stewart were strung up side by side.
> Directly in front of them, and within ten feet, was
> Aikens, in the same situation. A short time suf-
> ficed to divest me of my scanty Indian apparel and
> place me by the side of the latter. Thus we stood,
> or rather hung, Aikens and myself facing Stewart
> and Martin.
>
> Big Wolf and a number of his old men stationed
> themselves near us. Then a long line of warriors,
> of whom there were probably two hundred, moved
> forward slowly, silently, and in single file, with
> the leader of the war party at their head. Their
> pace was half walk, half shuffle, a spasmodic,
> nervous motion, like the artificial motion of figures
> in a puppet show. Each carried in one hand his
> knife or tomahawk, in the other a flint stone, three

inches or more in length and fashioned into the
shape of a sharp pointed arrow.

The head of the procession, as it circled a long
way round, first approached Stewart and Martin.
As it passed them, two of the youngest warriors
broke from the line, seized them by the hair, and
scalped them, then resumed their places and moved
on.   This operation consists of cutting off only a
portion of the skin which covers the skull, of the
dimensions of a silver dollar, and does not neces-
sarily destroy life.   Blood flowed from them in
profusion, running down over the face and trickling
from their long beards.

The warriors passed Aikens and myself without
harming us, marching round again in the same
order as before.   Up to this time there had been
entire silence, except a yell from the two young
men when in the act of scalping, but now the whole
party halted a half-minute and, slapping their hands
upon their mouths, united in an energetic war
whoop.   Then in silence the circuitous march was
continued.

When they reached Stewart and Martin the second
time, the sharp flint arrowheads were brought into
use.   Each man, as he passed, with a wild screech,
would brandish his tomahawk in their faces an instant, and then draw the sharp point of the stone
across their bodies.   By the time the line had
passed, our poor suffering companions presented
an awful spectacle.

Still they left Aikens and myself unharmed; nevertheless, we regarded it as certain that very soon
we should be subjected to similar tortures.   We
would have been devoutly thankful at that terrible
hour could we have been permitted to choose our
own mode of being put to death.

How many times they circled round, halting to
sound the war whoop, and going through the same
demoniac exercise, I cannot tell.   They persisted
in the hellish work until every inch of the bodies
of the unhappy men was hacked and covered with
clotted blood.

In the progress of their torture there occurred an intermission of some quarter of an hour. During this period, some threw themselves on the ground and lighted their pipes, others collected in little groups. All, however, laughed and shouted, pointing their fingers at the prisoners in derision, as if taunting them as cowards. The prisoners bore themselves differently. Stewart uttered not a word, but his sobs and groans were such as only the most intense pain and agony can wring from the human heart. The pitiful cries and prayers of Martin were unceasing. Constantly he was exclaiming: 'Oh! God have mercy on me!' 'Oh, Father in heaven, pity me!' 'Oh! Lord Jesus, come and put me out of pain!'

I hung down my head and closed my eyes to shut out the heartsickening scene before me. But this poor comfort was not vouchsafed me. They would grasp myself as well as Aikens by the hair, drawing our heads back violently, compelling us, however unwillingly, to stare directly at the agonized and writhing sufferers.

At the end of two hours the warriors halted and formed a half-circle. Two of them moved out from the center, striking into the war dance, raising the war song, advancing, receding, now moving to the right, now to the left, occupying ten minutes in proceeding as many paces. Finally, they reached the victims, danced before them for some time, then drew their hatchets suddenly and sent the bright blades crashing through their skulls. The bodies were taken down and rudely thrown aside upon the ground.

Aikens and myself now anticipated we would be compelled to suffer the same fate. To our astonishment, however, we were unbound, taken by separate guards, dressed in our hunting shirts and leggings, and started towards the camp.

As we moved off, I turned my head to take a last lingering look at my dead companions. The Indian dogs had already gathered round the corpses and were lapping the blood from their innumerable wounds. [7]

Captivity of Fanny Kelly

During the Civil War, thousands of people from northern states rolled westward in wagon trains.   In 1864 one of
these wagons contained a nineteen-year-old bride named Fanny
Kelly, her husband, and a small adopted daughter.   She was
a native of Canada but grew up in Kansas.   Soon after she
married Josiah Kelly, they decided to move to Idaho.   They
had not gone far when Fanny was captured by the Sioux.

The Indians carried Mrs. Kelly to their village which
was three hundred miles to the north.   There she was taken
by the aged chief, Silver Horn, to live with his six wives.
She was not molested by the chief because of his age and was
generally well treated by the women.   Then General Alfred
Sully invaded the Sioux country and drove the Indians into the
badlands.   Many warriors were killed and the tribe sought
revenge on their white captive.   Mrs. Kelly described what
happened in a fascinating narrative which was published after
her redemption.

> The next morning I could see that something un-
> usual was about to happen.   Notwithstanding the
> early hour, the sun scarcely appearing above the
> horizon, the principal chiefs and warriors were as-
> sembled in council, where, judging from the grave
> and reflective expression of their countenances,
> they were about to discuss some serious question.
>
> I had reason for apprehension, from their unfriendly
> manner toward me, and feared for the penalty I
> might soon have to pay.
>
> Soon they sent an Indian to me, who asked me if I
> was ready to die--to be burned at the stake.   I
> told him whenever Wakon-Tonka (the Great Spirit)
> was ready, he would call for me, and then I would
> be ready and willing to go.   He said that he had
> been sent from the council to warn me, that it had
> become necessary to put me to death, on account
> of my white brothers killing so many of their young
> men recently.   He repeated that they were not
> cruel for the pleasure of being so; necessity is
> their first law, and he and the wise chiefs, faithful
> to their hatred for the white race, were in haste to
> satisfy their thirst for vengeance; and, further, that
> the interest of their nation required it.

As soon as the chiefs were assembled around the council fire, the pipe-carrier entered the circle, holding in his hand the pipe ready lighted. Bowing to the four cardinal points, he uttered a short prayer, or invocation, and then presented the pipe to the old chief, Ottawa, but retained the bowl in his hand. When all the chiefs and men had smoked, one after the other, the pipebearer emptied the ashes into the fire, saying, 'Chiefs of the great Dakota nation, Wakon-Tonka give you wisdom, so that whatever be your determination, it may be conformable to justice.' Then, after bowing respectfully, he retired.

A moment of silence followed, in which every one seemed to be meditating seriously upon the words that had just been spoken. At length one of the most aged of the chiefs, whose body was furrowed with the scars of innumerable wounds, and who enjoyed among his people a reputation for great wisdom, arose.

Said he, 'The pale faces, our eternal persecutors, pursue and harass us without intermission, forcing us to abandon to them, one by one, our best hunting grounds, and we are compelled to seek a refuge in the depths of these Bad Lands, like timid deer. Many of them even dare to come into prairies which belong to us, to trap beaver, and hunt elk and buffalo, which are our property. These faithless creatures, the outcasts of their own people, rob and kill us when they can. Is it just that we should suffer these wrongs without complaining? Shall we allow ourselves to be slaughtered like timid Assinneboines, without seeking to avenge ourselves? Does not the law of the Dakotas say, Justice to our nation, and death to all pale faces? Let my brothers say if that is just,' pointing to the stake that was being prepared for me.

'Vengeance is allowable,' sententiously remarked Mahpeah (The Sky).

Another old chief, Ottawa, arose and said, 'It is the undoubted right of the weak and oppressed; and yet it ought to be proportioned to the injury received. Then why should we put this young, innocent

woman to death? Has she not always been kind to
us, smiled upon us, and sang for us? Do not all
our children love her as a tender sister? Why,
then, should we put her to so cruel a death for the
crimes of others, if they are of her nation? Why
should we punish the innocent for the guilty?

I looked to Heaven for mercy and protection, offering up those earnest prayers that are never offered
in vain; and oh! how thankful I was when I knew
their decision was to spare my life. Though terrible were my surroundings, life always became
sweet to me, when I felt that I was about to part
with it. 8

Experiences of Nick Wilson

    E. N. (Nick) Wilson was born in 1842 in Illinois. In
1850 his parents moved by ox cart to Grantsville, Utah, where
they established a sheep ranch. Some Gosiute Indians worked
on the ranch and Nick learned their language. He was deeply
distressed by the death of an Indian boy and in later life he
wrote in his life story that he loved him as much as if he
had been his own brother.

    After Pantsuk died, I had to herd the sheep by my-
self. The summer wore along very lonely for me,
until about the first of August, when a band of
Shoshone Indians came and camped near where I
was watching my sheep. Some of them could talk
the Gosiute language, which I had learned from my
little Indian brother. The Indians seemed to take
quite a fancy to me, and they would be with me
every chance they could get. They said they liked
to hear me talk their language, for they had never
heard a white boy talk it as well as I could.

One day an Indian rode up to the place where I was
herding. He had with him a little pinto pony. I
thought it was the prettiest animal I ever saw. The
Indian could talk Gosiute very well. He asked me
if I did not want to ride.... The next day he came
again with the pony and let me ride it. Several
other Indians were with him.... They kept coming
and giving me this fun for several days.

One day, after I had ridden till I was tired, I
brought the pony back to the Indian who had first
come, and he asked me if I did not want to keep it.

'I would rather have that pony, ' I replied, 'than anything else in the world. '

'You may have it, ' he said, 'if you will go away
with us. '

I told him I was afraid to go. He said he would
take good care of me and would give me bows and
arrows and all the buckskin clothes I needed.   I
asked him what they had to eat. He said they had
all kinds of meat, and berries, and fish, sage
chickens, ducks, geese, and rabbits.   This sounded
good to me. It surely beat living on 'lumpy dick'
and greens, our usual pioneer fare.

'Our papooses do not have to work, ' he went on,
'they have heap fun all the time, catching fish and
hunting and riding ponies. '

That looked better to me than herding a bunch of
sheep alone....   The next day I told them I would
go.

My parents knew nothing about it.   They would
never have consented to my going.   And it did look
like a foolish, risky thing to do; but I was lonely
and tired and hungry for excitement, and I yielded
to the temptation.   In five days the Indians were to
start north to join the rest....   I went with them,
and for two years I did not see a white man.   This
was in August, 1854.   I was just about twelve years
old at the time.

The Shoshones took Nick to their chief, the celebrated
Washakie, and he lived in his lodge as a brother.   His adopted
mother (Washakie's mother), was very kind to him.   He
learned in time that her two youngest sons had been buried
alive in a snowslide and she had dreamed that one of them
would return to her as a white child.   Washakie did not want
war with the whites and refused to allow his tribe to capture
a white child, but he had consented to the plan to try to persuade Nick to join them voluntarily.

Nick enjoyed his life with the tribe but at times he felt an urge to return to his white family. When Pocatello's band came in with white people's scalps he became enraged and wished he had never left home.

"My Indian mother was as good and kind to me as any one could be," he said, "but she did not seem to realize that there was another loving mother miles and miles away whose heart was sorrowing. . . .

"My Indian mother would often ask me a good many questions about my white mother. She asked me if I did not want to go home. I told her that I should like to see my folks very much, but if I went home they would keep me there, and I did not want to herd sheep. ' . . . and I love you too. If I went away you could not go with me; so taking it all around I should rather stay with you. ' "[9]

Nick lived two years with the Indians and became strongly attached to their way of life. When they fought Indian enemies he wanted to join in the battle. However, he was old enough when he joined the Shoshones to regard their customs with a certain amount of critical discrimination. Therefore he was only partially assimilated. [10]

Eventually Washakie sent him home to his family in order to avoid trouble with the whites. He did not wish to go and he promised his Indian mother that he would return at the first opportunity. But he was persuaded to become a Pony Express rider, a life which he liked, and gradually lost his desire to return to the Indians. Once his Indian mother came to Grantsville looking for him, but he was away. She was cordially received by his white mother and stayed with her for two months, but when he did not come home she returned to the mountains. When he learned of this visit he went in search of her and found that she had died. He and Washakie remained lifelong friends. [11]

Conclusions

Based on the foregoing narratives and others, it would seem that the treatment of captives varied considerably in different native American culture areas, particularly between eastern and western tribes. This is to be expected because of the tremendous differences in culture traits among tribes and regions.

In all regions, however, caprice was a major factor which frequently determined a captive's fate. Death, servitude, or adoption depended upon the whim of the warrior who first touched the captive. If a relative had been killed recently, the warrior might take revenge by tomahawking the first white person to fall into his hands. But if his grief had had time to subside he might save the captive as a replacement. The threat of death hung over most captives until they were adopted, and even afterward if they proved to be unsatisfactory substitutes.

The treatment of captive children seems to have been similar in initial stages, both east and west of the Mississippi. Most children were treated brutally at the time of capture. Babies and toddlers usually were killed immediately and other small children would be dispatched during the rapid retreat to the Indian villages if they cried, failed to keep the pace, or otherwise indicated a lack of fortitude needed to become a worthy member of the tribe. Upon reaching the village, the child might face such ordeals as running the gauntlet or dancing in the center of a throng of threatening Indians. The prisoner might be so seriously injured at this time that he would no longer be acceptable for adoption. 12

The adoption ceremony completely changed the child's status. In the Eastern Woodlands, adoption of children usually followed quickly after capture. In the eyes of their adopted families, these children were as deserving of kind treatment as were the deceased relatives they replaced. Life was less arduous in the semi-sedentary villages east of the Mississippi and, except when warfare brought devastation, the captive child probably did not have to work harder than he would have with his white family. The narratives of such captives as David Boyd indicate that genuine affection developed between the Indian family and the adopted captive.

West of the Mississippi the life of captive children was more difficult. Tribes dependent upon hunting or gathering for subsistence, such as those of the Plains, West, and Southwest (the Pueblos excepted), frequently experienced hunger, especially when hard-pressed by enemies. During such times, captives were the last to be fed and the first to be blamed for tribal misfortune.

Adoption of white captives was frequently delayed in the West and the children served their masters as menials. The sale or trade of captive children from one tribe or band

to another was more frequent among western Indians, and
the opportunity for affection to develop was delayed.

Probably few children suffered more than a thirteen-
year-old Texas girl named Matilda Lockhart who was captured
by Comanches in 1838. When redeemed two years later, she
was barely recognizable by her parents. Battered and covered with sores, her nose burned off to the bone, she related that if she fell asleep the Indians would wake her by
"sticking a chunk of fire to her flesh, especially to her
nose."[13]

In regard to the treatment of white female captives
taken beyond the age of puberty, a distinct difference is indicated between eastern and western tribes. The seventeenth-
century New England captive, Mary Rowlandson, pointed out
that white women were in little danger of sexual abuse: "...
though I was gone from home, and met with all sorts of Indians ... and there being no Christian soul near me, yet not
one of them offered the least imaginable miscarriage to me."[14]

Among eastern Indians purificatory rites preceded and
followed raids, and sexual continence might be required of
warriors during extended periods of hostilities. This circumstance saved many a captured female from a fate which
she feared more than death. The Shawnees, for instance,
avoided violating women prisoners because it would anger the
Great Spirit.[15]

While forcible rape of white females by Indians east
of the Mississippi was rare or non-existent, women captured
as adults in that region frequently became the wives of warriors. It would be greatly enlightening if more information
were available regarding the force of pressure placed on
captive women to marry Indians. Francis Parkman has asserted that young women who refuse to marry Indians "are
treated with a singular forebearance, in which superstition,
natural temperament, and a sense of right and justice may
all claim a share."[16]

A case in point is that of Mrs. Hannah Dennis, a
young woman whose husband and baby were killed by Shawnees during a raid into Virginia in 1757. She protected herself by professing witchcraft and curing the sick. "In this
manner she conducted herself, 'till she became so great a
favorite with them that they gave her full liberty and honored
her as a queen."[17]

Dramatically different, however, was a case described by Mrs. Richard Bard, who was captured by Delawares in 1758. She met a woman from her home community who had been in captivity several years, had married an Indian, and had a child by him. Mrs. Bard "reproved her for this but received for answer, that before she had consented, they had tied her to a stake in order to burn her. She added, that as soon as their captive women could speak the Indian tongue, they were obliged to marry some one of them or be put to death. "[18]

It is evident that a strong deterrent to marrying a warrior was hatred of Indians by frontier people. Captive women knew that if they consorted with Indian men and later returned to their white families they would be disgraced. A case of this kind involved the Smith family of Mill Creek, western Virginia. Mrs. Smith and several of her children were captured in 1758. About three years later, Smith recovered his wife. She was married to a chief and had a child by him which she refused to abandon. Smith did not abuse his wife but he hated the child. The boy ran away to rejoin the Indians as soon as he became old enough. [19]

The lives of women held by eastern Indians probably were no more arduous than those of the average pioneer woman. Some of them may have preferred the wild, free life style of the Indian to the "irksome restraints of society." It is possible, also, that some were better treated by the Indians than by their white families. The Indians believed this to be the case and some white captive women east of the Mississippi lent credence to the claim by their actions if not by their words. When the Moravian missionary, Christian Frederick Post, was sent on a peace-making mission to the Delawares, he received a lecture by Shingas, a chief who terrified the Pennsylvania frontier: "We love you more than you love us; for, when we take any prisoners from you, we treat them as our own.... We are poor, and we cloathe them as well as we can, though you see our own children are as naked as the first. "[20]

In August 1762 a large number of captives were surrendered at Lancaster. An Iroquois named Thomas King spoke as follows on that occasion:

You have told us of the Six Nations that we must assist you to see your flesh and blood. We have done what we can.... I have got a great many of

them, though at first with great difficulty. When I
brought them by the English forts they took them
away from me. ... they got them from me, and
I believe they have made servants of them. This
is the reason why I brought so few of them. No
wonder they are so loath to come, when you make
servants of them. I brought a girl to Easton, and
she ran away. When I came home, I found her
there. 'Bless me, ' says I, 'There is my wife. I
was sorry that I had delivered her, but to my surprise I found her at home. You know it is hard to
part with a wife. Brother, I have brought an English prisoner (the girl mentioned), whom I love as
my own wife. I have a young child by her. You
know it is hard for a man to part with his wife. I
have delivered her. Therefore, take care of her
and keep her safe. [21]

As a general rule, women were not burned at the
stake in eastern North America, death by this means being
considered an honor reserved for warriors. Occasionally,
however, if Indians were inflamed with a desire to avenge
deaths of relatives and no male captives were available, a
woman might be put to the torture. Such a fate befell Mrs.
James Moore and her sixteen-year-old daughter, Jane, in
1784. To compensate for the loss of two warriors the Indians lashed the captives to a post and burned them to death
by thrusting flaming pine splinters into their flesh. [22]

West of the Mississippi, white women captives led a
precarious existence. Frequently they were subjected to
sexual abuse. Carl Coke Rister has written that a female
captive became the property of the first warrior who laid
hands on her and that he might sell her to anyone who
wanted her. Besides becoming a drudge in the lodge she usually was compelled to submit to sexual advances. "Because
of this well known fact, " Rister asserted, "white women
along the frontier generally regarded death as preferable to
captivity. "[23]

In 1865 James Box, a Texas rancher, was killed by
Kiowas and his wife and four daughters captured. The Indians brained the youngest daughter against a tree when she
wouldn't stop crying. Ida, aged 7, was tortured but not sex-
ually abused. Mrs. Box and her two teen-aged daughters
were outraged by the raiders. [24]

It is of note that most white women redeemed from captivity in the West charged that sexual abuse of their fellow captives was common but claimed that because of some unusual circumstance they, themselves, had been spared the ordeal. An exception was the case of the wife and daughter of the Ute agent, M. C. Meeker, both of whom reluctantly acknowledged that they had been raped the night following the attack on the agency and the murder of their husband and father. [25]

West of the Mississippi, there were few if any instances of white females captured beyond the age of puberty who willingly became the wives of warriors. After being compelled to do so, however, they sometimes chose to remain with an Indian husband. In 1838 the Santa Fe trader, Josiah Gregg, detected a Mexican woman among the Comanches. She had been kidnapped from the home of the Governor of Chihuahua. A reward of $1,000 had been offered by her father but she refused to leave her captors. "She sent word to her father that they had disfigured her by tattooing; that she was married ..., and that she would be made more unhappy by returning to her father under these circumstances than by remaining where she was. "[26]

The treatment of mature male white captives was similar in most North American tribes. A man who fell into Indian hands was considered to have forfeited his life. Usually he would be killed immediately, but in other instances he would be taken to the captors' village and tortured to death. [27]

Nathaniel Knowles has pointed out in a perceptive article that Indians gained great emotional satisfaction from prolonged tortures inflicted on captives. "Such behavior, " he asserts, "must be evaluated in terms of motivations imposed by the various cultures of the several tribes, particularly with respect to the social and religious connotations of the war patterns. " Knowles called attention to the forgotten fact that many of the most cruel forms of torture, such as burning at the stake, were introduced to the Indians by Europeans. [28]

Mature white male captives were occasionally adopted by Indians east of the Mississippi, especially if they were formidable adversaries, in the hope that they could be persuaded to become warriors. Adoption of grown white prisoners apparently was seldom attempted by western Indians.

In all western native culture areas, white men who were
captured almost invariably were killed except on the Northwest Coast.   In that unique culture area true slavery existed.
Male captives sometimes were saved because of their value
as property in this most property-conscious of all Indian
societies.

Having concluded that there were regional differences
in the treatment of captive white women and children and, to
a smaller degree, of men, consideration will be given to the
question of whether such differences affected assimilation to
a significant extent.

Based upon the narratives quoted, as well as others
too numerous to include, it appears that rarely did a child
successfully resist assimilation in any native culture area.
In the Ultra-Mississippi area, early adoption of children led
to strong ties of affection.   This circumstance probably
smoothed the course of assimilation.

In the West, Southwest, and Plains culture areas, captive children were treated brutally for a considerable period
of time.   Adoption might be delayed indefinitely while the
child was traded from one band to another.   In most cases,
however, the captive eventually would be assigned to Indians
who treated him with sufficient kindness for him to consider
his new surroundings a deliverance from previous ordeals.
Evidence gleaned from primary sources indicates that at this
point in the captive's life, assimilation began to develop at a
much more rapid rate.   The conclusion is reached, therefore, that brutal treatment of captive children delayed their
assimilation but did not prevent it.

The assimilation of white adults was a great deal more
difficult than the Indianization of children.   In regard to captives among eastern tribes, it has not been possible in the
course of this study to determine how frequently women captured above the age of puberty rejected an opportunity to return home.   In the surrender of prisoners to Bouquet's army,
the fact that some of the women showing reluctance to be
redeemed had both white and half-Indian children proves that
they had been captured as adults and had submitted to Indian
marriages.   Yet this is scarcely conclusive evidence as to
the degree of assimilation attained.   They may have loved
their warrior husbands and been reluctant to part with their
mixed-blood children.   On the other hand, they may
have feared ostracism if they returned to white civilization.

Among western Indian tribes much more positive conclusions can be drawn as to the assimilation of mature white
female captives.   Very few, if any, of them became Indianized.   Unlike eastern captives who lived in the lodges of
semi-sedentary Indians, these western frontier women were
held by tribes which wandered much of the time in pursuit of
the buffalo.   Hardships inherent in this mode of life, coupled
with sexual and other forms of abuse, were more than most
of these women could bear.   Death seemed preferable to acceptance of the Indian way of life, and most of them died.

It is concluded that the difference in treatment of women prisoners in various culture areas played only a minor
role in the assimilation process.   West of the Mississippi,
women resisted Indianization or died in the attempt.   In the
East, it is obvious that most captive women retained the desire to return to their white families and, indeed, more
proof is needed before it can be said that any of them became
thoroughly assimilated.

Assimilation of men captives was rare.   Most mature
men captured by Indians were killed.   There were exceptions,
however, particularly east of the Mississippi.   During Colonial and Revolutionary times many men captives, as well as
women and children, were sold to the French in Canada or
to the British at Detroit.   Others, chiefly renegades or out-
laws, who fell into Indian hands convinced their captors that
they would fight against the whites.   The notorious Girty
brothers spent a part of their childhood as captives and returned to the Indians years later as British agents, leading
raids into Kentucky.   Less widely known was the case of
Timothy Dorman.   He had been an outlaw in England before
coming to the frontier of western Virginia.   When he was
captured by Indians near Buchannon Fort he joined them in
attacks against his former neighbors.   Once he led the Indians across the Allegheny Mountains and attacked the Gregg
family for whom he had formerly worked.   A daughter of the
family was captured and Dorman tomahawked and scalped
her. [29]

In a few cases, eastern tribes preserved the life of a
white man renowned for his exploits against them in the hope
that they could make an Indian of him.   Perhaps the most
famous case of this kind was the captivity of Daniel Boone,
in 1778, by the Shawnee chief, Blackfish.   So confident was
Blackfish of the superiority of Indian civilization that he believed even Boone could be assimilated.   Boone used this

circumstance to advantage in saving the lives of thirty companions who likewise fell into Blackfish's grasp while making
salt at the Blue Licks, in Kentucky. With this remarkable
speech he convinced the Indians that he could persuade the
entire settlement of Boonesborough to adopt the Indian way of
life:

> Brothers! What I have promised you, I can much
> better fulfil in the spring than now; then the wea-
> ther will be warm, & the women & children can
> travel from Boonesborough to the Indian towns, and
> all live with you as one people.   You have got all
> the young men; to kill them, as has been suggested,
> would displease the Great Spirit, & you could not
> then expect future success in hunting or war; and
> if you spare them they will make you fine warriors,
> and excellent hunters to kill game for your squaws
> and children.   These young men have done you no
> harm; ... spare them and the Great Spirit will
> smile upon you. [30]

Boone's oratory prevented an attack on the settlement.
Taken to the Indian village, the salt makers, with one exception, eventually escaped or were bought by the British.
Boone became Blackfish's adopted son and gave every indication of contentment with Indian life.   But when he detected
that the Shawnees were going to raid Kentucky, he escaped
and returned to Boonesborough in time to prepare the fort
for defense.   Before the siege of Boonesborough began,
Blackfish still believed that his adopted son loved him and
had returned to the settlement only for the purpose of fulfilling his promise to bring the white people to live with the
Indians.   In regard to Boone's assimilation, Blackfish was
mistaken, but he was not entirely incorrect in his belief in
the attractions of Indian life.   One member of the salt-mak-
ing party lived out the rest of his life as an Indian. [31] He
was one of the very few mature white male captives successfully assimilated by either the eastern or western Indians.

Notes

1.   John D. Hunter, Manners and Customs of Several Indian
       Tribes Located West of the Mississippi. (Minneapo-
       lis, 1957), 12-35.

2.   John Rodgers Jewitt, The Headhunters of Nootka, in

Frederick Drimmer, Scalps and Tomahawks. (New York, 1961), 216-55.

3. Carl Coke Rister, Comanche Bondage. (Glendale, 1955).

4. Howard H. Peckham, Captured by Indians. (New Brunswick, 1954), 195-98.

5. J. P. Dunn, Jr., Massacres of the Mountains. (New York, n. d.), 146-64.

6. R. B. Stratton, Captivity of the Oatman Girls. (New York, 1858), 231.

7. Lee, Three Years Among the Comanches, 149-57.

8. Kelly, Narrative of My Captivity, 107-09.

9. E. N. Wilson, The White Indian Boy. (Yonkers, 1919), 1, 8-9, 15, 25, 39-41.

10. Swanton, "Notes on the Mental Assimilation of Races, " 498.

11. Wilson, The White Indian Boy, 117-18, 140, 192-96.

12. Nathaniel Knowles, "The Torture of Captives by the Indians of Eastern North America, " in American Philosophical Society Proceedings, LXXXII, (1940), 151-225.

13. Rister, Border Captives, 87.

14. Mary Rowlandson, Narrative of Captivity of Mary Rowlandson. (Boston, 1930), 33.

15. Knowles, "The Torture of Captives, " 153, 177, 207.

16. Francis Parkman, The Conspiracy of Pontiac. (New York, 1929), 364.

17. Alexander Scott Withers, Chronicles of Border Warfare. (Parsons, W. Va., 1961), 89-93.

18. Archibald Bard, An Account of the Captivity of Richard Bard, in Archibald Loudon, A Selection of Some of the Most Interesting Narratives of Outrages Committed by the Indians. (Carlisle, 1808), II, 52.

19. Willis DeHass, History of the Early Settlement and In-
     dian Wars of Western Virginia. (Wheeling, 1851),
     205-06.

20. C. Hale Sipe, The Indian Wars of Pennsylvania. (Har-
     risburg, 1931), 363.

21. Ibid. , 825-26.

22. Withers, Chronicles of Border Warfare, 374.

23. Rister, Border Captives, 25.

24. Ibid. , 51.

25. Robert Emmitt, The Last War Trail. (Norman, 1954),
     210-14.

26. Rister, Border Captives, 51.

27. Hodge, Handbook of American Indians, I, 204.

28. Knowles, "The Torture of Captives, " 151.

29. Withers, Chronicles of Border Warfare, 341-43.

30. Draper MSS. , 11 C:62, quoting Joseph Jackson, a sur-
     vivor of the party (Wisconsin Historical Society).

31. Bakeless, Daniel Boone, 176.

Chapter 7

TIME REQUIRED TO BECOME AN INDIAN

It would seem obvious that a major factor affecting assimilation of captives was the length of time held. And certainly, if other factors were equal, a long captivity was more likely to lead to Indianization than a short one. But persuasive evidence exists that some captives were held by the Indians many years without losing the desire to escape, while others adopted their new way of life in a matter of months.

There is some indication that the traumatic experience of seizure by Indians may have shocked small children so severely as to deprive them of memory of their earlier lives. In January 1836 a family named Hibbons was attacked by Comanches in Texas. The father and an infant were killed while the mother and a three-year-old boy were captured. Mrs. Hibbons escaped during the first night and found a Texas Ranger camp the following afternoon. The Rangers located the Indians within twenty-four hours and rescued the child. Noah Smithwick, a Ranger who witnessed the scene, observed that although the little boy had been in captivity only two days he was "too much dazed and bewildered by the many strange scenes through which it had passed so rapidly, to even know its mother.... "[1]

A somewhat similar situation occurred as a result of the Box family captivity previously mentioned. Ida Box was seven years old when captured by Kiowas. Because she could not understand their commands the squaws compelled her to walk barefooted on live coals. When rescued after only ten weeks of captivity she had almost forgotten the English language. [2]

The following case histories are illustrative of the degree of assimilation attained by captives remaining with Indians for brief periods.

Captivity of Anna Metzger

Anna Metzger was the daughter of Peter Metzger, a
German who settled in Gillespie County, Texas.   In 1864 she
was captured by Kiowa Indians and witnessed the murder of
her sister.   She was eleven years old at the time.   She remained with the tribe only nine months before being redeemed
by a trader.   She described her experiences as follows:

> ... the squaws and younger Indians were taking
> turns in beating me and lacerating my flesh in a
> manner most distressing.   At last my face was
> painted, a clout of buffalo skin was put upon me,
> and it seemed that I had been formally initiated
> into the tribe.   After this I was ... to be a serv-
> ant.   That night I was given a buffalo skin for a
> bed, and it was gratefully received after so much
> mistreatment. [3]

Anna was assigned as a servant to the chief's two
wives, one of whom treated her cruelly and the other kindly.
One of her tasks was to look after the Indian children.   "The
older ones chattered to me, " she recalled, "and I readily
learned their language.   ... there was a little Indian girl who
was an unswerving friend of mine....   In all my troubles she
showed her devotion, though often at the cost of a severe
beating to herself.   I shall never forget her words of healing
sympathy at times when they were so much needed by me. "

Anna retained a strong desire to return home and
risked death to run away from the Indians to a trader's house.
Nevertheless, it is a remarkable fact that in less than a year
she learned the Indian language and almost forgot her own.
"I had forgotten my language to a great extent, " she ad-
mitted, "understanding what my brother ... said, but in some
ways I could not speak the German words.   I made myself
understood by means of gestures.   In this I had become very
proficient. "[3]

Captivity of Santiago McKinn

Santiago McKinn was captured by the famous Apache
raider, Geronimo, in 1885.   When Geronimo surrendered in
March 1886, the boy was brought in.   Although he had been
with the Apaches less than a year he had already become
thoroughly assimilated.   Charles F. Lummis, scholar and

newspaper editor, was present and described the scene:

> The poor child, scaly with dirt, wild as a coyote,
> made my eyes a bit damp. He is a pathetic case.
> One day last summer Geronimo and his band
> swooped down upon a little ranch on the Miembres
> River, above Deming, New Mexico. They did not
> attack the house, but skimmed along the ridge,
> where the two McKinn boys were herding cattle.
> The elder was killed, as nearly as we can learn,
> and Santiago, now eleven years old, was carried
> off. He has been with the Apaches ever since. But
> that is not what seems so pitiful. He has had to
> share their long marches, their scanty and uninvit-
> ing fare, and all the hardships of such a life, no
> doubt; but he has not been maltreated. The Apaches
> are kind to their children, and have been kind to
> him. The sorrow is that he has become so abso-
> lutely Indianized.
>
> It was almost impossible to get hold of him in
> camp. The Indian boys liked to be talked with; but
> let a white man approach, and Santiago would be
> off instanter. He understands English and Spanish
> (his father is Irish, his mother a Mexican), but it
> was hard labor to get him to speak either. Yes-
> terday General Crook had an Apache bring him to
> Major and Mrs. Roberts' house. When told that he
> was to be taken back to his father and mother, San-
> tiago began boo-hooing with great vigor. He said
> in Apache--for the little rascal has already become
> rather fluent in that language--that he didn't want to
> go back. He wanted to stay with the Indians. All
> sorts of rosy pictures of the delights of home were
> drawn, but he would have none of them, and acted
> like a wild young animal in a trap. When they
> lifted him into the wagon which was to take him to
> the station, he renewed his wails, and was still at
> them as he disappeared from view. [4]

Captivity of T. A. (Dot) Babb

In September 1865, Comanches raided the Babb ranch
in Wise County, Texas, killed Mrs. Babb, and took the boy
prisoner. He was thirteen years old. Early in his captivity
he tried to escape. Caught and threatened with death, he was

spared because of a brave show of defiance.   After a year of
captivity he was adopted into the tribe and taken on raids
against other Indians.   He enjoyed the wild, free life, but he
did not forget his white family and managed to send word of
his situation to his father.

Through the intercession of Chief Esserhaby, he was
given his choice of remaining a Comanche or returning to his
white relatives: "Chief Horseback and many of his band were
confident that after I had habituated myself so unreservedly to
Indian life, I would elect to stay with them, " he wrote in a
narrative of his captivity.   "However, in this they were in
great error, as my decision was instant and unalterable to
return as quickly as possible to my father and kindred. "

Restored in 1867, he kept in touch with his Comanche
friends.   He visited them on the reservation from time to
time.   On one occasion he claimed land in the Indian Territory as a member of the tribe and took his white family to
live there for a brief period. [5]

Captivity of Frank Buckelew

Frank Buckelew was born in Louisiana in 1852.   Or-
phaned at an early age, he went to live with a sister on the
Sabinal River in western Texas.   He was almost fourteen
years old when captured by Lipan Indians.   Their war chief,
Custaleta, could speak English and Frank told him he was
only ten years old in the hope that they would spare his life.
Custaleta told him that if he were English they would kill him
but if he were German they would let him live.   Frank, who
had already lied about his age, refused to deny his English
ancestry and his brave show of defiance won Custaleta's ad-
miration.   He was carried into captivity in Mexico and remained with the Lipans eleven months before managing to
escape.

Although Buckelew never lost his desire to leave the
Indians and risked death to escape it is evident that he acquired some traits of Indian culture.   At first he was re-
pulsed by their manner of eating but in a short time he began
to enjoy his meals, including raw liver.   He soon became
expert in the use of the bow and arrow.   More significantly,
he rapidly developed an attachment for Custaleta, the chief
who treated him kindly. [6]

Captivity of Pierre Esprit Radisson

Pierre Esprit Radisson, a sixteen-year-old French Canadian, was captured by Mohawks while duck hunting near the frontier post of Three Rivers, Quebec, in the spring of 1652. He wounded some warriors before they overpowered him. When one of the Indians attacked him, Pierre gave him a beating with his fists. Impressed by his bravery, they painted him like an Indian and treated him well.

After slightly more than a year of captivity, during which he became considerably Indianized, he escaped and wrote a fascinating account of his adventures.

> In the same cabin that I was, there has been a wild man (Indian) wounded with a small shot. I thought I have seen him the day of my taking, which made me fear lest I was the one that wounded him. He knowing it to be so had showed me as much charity as a Christian might have given. Another of his fellows (I also wounded) came to me at my first coming there, whom I thought to have come for revenge, contrariwise showed me a cheerful countenance, he gave me a box full of red paintings, calling me his brother.

> The next day we marched into a village where as we came in sight we heard nothing but outcrys, as from one side, as from the other, being a quarter mile from the village. They sat down and I in the middle, where I saw women and men and children with staves and in array, which put me in fear, and instantly stripped me naked. My keeper gave me a sign to be gone as fast as I could. In the meanwhile many of the village came about us, among which a good old woman, and a boy with a hatchet in his hand came near me. The old woman covered me, and the young man took me by the hand and led me out of the company. The old woman made me step aside from those that were ready to strike at me. ... I escaped the blows. Then they brought me into their cottage, there the old woman showed me kindness. She gave me to eat. The great terror I had a little before took my stomach away. I stayed an hour, where a great company of people came to see me. Here came a company of old men, having pipes in their mouths, sat about me.

After smoking, they led me into another cabin,
where there were a company all smoking, they made
me sit down by the fire, which made me apprehend
they should cast me into the said fire. But it proved
otherwise; for the old woman followed me ... then
took her girdle and about me she tied it, so brought
me to her cottage, and made [me] sit down.... Then
she began to dance and sing awhile, after she brings
down from her box a comb, gives it to a maid that
was near me, who presently comes to grease and
comb my hair, and took away the paint that the
fellows stuck to my face.   Now the old woman gets
me some Indian corn toasted in the fire.   ... after
this she gave me a blue coverlet, stockings and
shoes, and wherewith to make me drawers.   She
looked in my clothes, and if she found any lice she
would squeeze them betwixt her teeth, as if they
had substantial meet.   I stayed with her son, who
took me from those of my first takers, and got at
last a great acquaintance with many.   I did what I
could to get familiarity with them, yet I suffered
no wrong at their hands, taking all freedom, which
the old woman inticed me to do.   But still they al-
tered my face wherever I went, and I a new dish to
satisfy nature.

I took all the pleasures imaginable, having a small
piece at my command, shooting partridges and
squirrels, playing most part of the day with my
companions.   The old woman wished that I would
make myself more familiar with her 2 daughters
which were tolerable among such people.   They
were accustomed to grease and comb my hair in
the morning. I went with them into the wilderness,
there they would be gabbling which I could not understand.   They wanted no company but I was sure
to be of the number. I brought always some gifts
that I received, which I gave to my pursekeeper
and refuge, the good old woman.   I lived 5 weeks
without thinking from whence I came.   I learned
more of their manners in 6 weeks than if I had
been in France 6 months.   At the end I was
troubled in mind which made her inquire if I was
Anjonack, a Huron word.   At this I made as if I
were supported for speaking in a strange language,
which she liked well, calling me by the name of her
son who before was killed....   She inquired of me

whether I was Afferony, a French.   I answering
no, saying I was Panugaga, that is, of their nation,
for which she was pleased.

After his adoption into the tribe Radisson went on a
hunting expedition with three Mohawk warriors and a Huron
captive.   That night the Huron proposed to him that they kill
the three Mohawks and escape.   Radisson was reluctant, but

at last I consented, considering they were mortal
enemies to my country, that had cut the throats of
so many of my relations, burned and murdered
them.   I promised him to succour him in his de-
sign.   They not understanding our language asked
the Algonquin what is that that he said, but told
them some other story, nor did they suspect us in
the least.   Their belly full, their mind without
care, wearied to the utmost ... fell asleep secure-
ly, leaning their arms up and down without the
least danger.   Then my wild man pushed me, thinking I was asleep.   He rises and sits him down by
the fire, beholding them one after another, and
taking their arms aside, and having the hatchets in
his hand gives me one; to tell the truth I was
loathsome to do them mischief that never did me
any.   Yet for the above said reasons I took the
hatchet and began the execution, which was soon
done.

They fled in a canoe, Radisson feeling great remorse
over killing the Indians.   Fourteen days later they were overtaken at St. Peter's Lake.   The Huron was killed and his
heart eaten by the Mohawks.   Radisson expected a similar
fate.

On the return to the village, the prisoner was tormented with burning brands and told to make ready for the
final torture.   But suddenly his Indian "parents" appeared.
"The mother pushes in among the crew directly to me, and
when she was near enough, she clutches hold of my hair as
one desperate, calling me often by my name; drawing me out
of my rank, she puts me into the hands of her husband, who
then bid me have courage, conducting me on another way
home to his cabin, when he made me sit down.   He said to
me: You senseless, thou was my son, and thou rendered
thyself enemy, thy lovest not thy mother, nor thy father that
gave thee thy life.... "

Soon some warriors tied him to a scaffold. There he was tormented by men, women and children, had a finger crushed and burning brands pressed to his flesh. He saw several of his fellow prisoners tortured to death, including a French woman who had an unborn child torn from her body and was forced to eat part of it. The next day he was taken to a council where his adopted parents bargained for his life.

> My father sings awhile; so done, makes a speech, and taking the porcelaine necklace from off me throws it at the feet of an old man, and cuts the cord that held me, then makes me rise. The joy that I received at that time was incomparable, for suddenly my pains and griefs ceased, makes me sing, to which I consented with all my heart. Whilst I did sing they hooped and hollowed on all sides. ... Now I see myself free from death.

Radisson resumed the life he had led before his escape. His adopted father then began urging him to become a warrior.

> The desire that I had to make me beloved, for the assurance of my life made me resolve to offer myself for to serve.... I ventured to ask him what I was. He presently answers that I was an Iroquois as himself. Let me revenge, said I, my kindred. I love my brother. Let me die with him. I would die with you, but you will not because you go against the French. Let me again go with my brother, the prisoners and the heads that I shall bring, to the joy of my mothers and sisters, will make me undertake at my return to take up the hatchet against those of Quebec, of the Three Rivers, and Montreal ... and that it's I that kills them, and by that you will know that I am your son, worthy to bear that title that you gave me when I adopted you.

He went on a raiding party with ten warriors. In the area of the Great Lakes, they fell upon a small band of Indians, killing men, women, and children. They took some women prisoners but killed most of them when they could not keep the pace.

When they returned to their village, Radisson gave the two heads of Indians he had killed to his adopted sister. He gave a female prisoner to his mother to be her slave. "This voyage being ended, albeit I came to this village & twice with fear and terror, the 3d time notwithstanding with joy and contentment. "

Radisson went with some Iroquois on a visit to the Dutch city of Orange.   There the governor offered to purch- ase his freedom but he "accepted not, for several reasons. The one was for not to be beholding to them, and the other being loathsome to leave such kind of good people.   For then I began to love my new parents that were so good and so favorable to me.   The 3d reason was to watch a better op- portunity to retire to the French rather than make that long circuit.... "

Soon after returning to the Indian village he began to regret not having accepted the governor's offer.   "I was not 15 days returned, but that nature itself reproached me to lead such a life, remembering the sweet behavior and mildness of the French, and considered with myself what end could I ex- pect of such a barbarous nation, enemy to God and man. "

On August 29, 1653, he ran away and escaped to the Dutch.   After a brief visit to France he returned to Canada to become a famous explorer and trader among the tribes. [7]

Captivity of Martina Diaz (Martha Day)

Martina Diaz was captured by Comanche Indians in southern Texas.   She was sixteen years old when taken. She gained her freedom two years later with the assistance of Lawrie Tatum, an Indian agent who redeemed many captives. Held by a warrior named Black Beard, she feared for her life if she should attempt to escape.   Nevertheless, when her band came to the agency for rations she fled into the dark- ness and concealed herself on the front porch of the agency until morning.   Tatum reported that she told him "she had been captured in the vicinity of San Antonio about two years before, while on her way to school, " and she wanted to go home.   "I told her I was glad to see her and would send her there.   My wife ... had a busy day preparing clothing for her to take the place of the Comanche costume.   My quarters were closely guarded that day by the Indians, who apparently intended to shoot her if they got sight of her.   In the even- ing, when nicely dressed, she was a handsome young woman ... and happy with the thought of returning to her people.... "

Before leaving for home Martina told Tatum there were other Mexican captives in the Comanche camp who wished to escape from the Indians. With this information as a starting point Tatum recovered eleven boys and returned them to their families. [8]

Captivity of Christian Fast

During the American Revolution a Westmoreland County, Pennsylvania, youth named Christian Fast volunteered as a cavalryman. In June 1780 he was captured by Delaware Indians near the Falls of the Ohio. He behaved bravely and so impressed the Indians that an old warrior adopted him. After his adoption he was treated well and allowed to go hunting with an Indian brother. He was urged to marry a young Indian maiden but offered the excuse that he was not a skillful enough hunter to provide for her. By the end of his second year of captivity the Indians believed that he had adopted their way of life so thoroughly that they took him with them on a raid. They besieged the stockade at Wheeling for three days. On the third night he slipped away from the Indians and fled to Fort Ross to warn of an impending attack. When the Indians arrived at the fort he helped defend it against them. When he returned home he so nearly resembled an Indian that his parents were unable to recognize him. [9]

It would appear from the foregoing case studies that the length of time held in captivity was not the overriding factor in determining the degree of assimilation. As further evidence of this fact the following table, containing fifty captivities, is intended to illustrate the scattering of results when the length of time in captivity is the only factor considered:

Name	Years in Captivity	Degree of Assimilation
Hanson, Elizabeth	1	15%
Plummer, Rachel	1	0
Lockhart, Matilda	2	0
Putnam (girl)	2	90
Bradley, Isaac	2	30
Girty, Simon	3	40
Girty, James	3	50

Name	Years in Captivity	Degree of Assimilation
Girty, George	3	60%
Boyd, Thomas	4	55
Leininger, Barbara	4	20
LeRoy, Marie	4	20
Lytle, Eleanor	4	50
Smith, James	4	20
Friend, Temple	5	90
Gibson, Hugh	5	15
Moxie, John Valentine	5	90
Oatman, Olive	5	15
Smith, Clinton	5	90
Dennis, Hannah	6	15
Grouard, Frank	6	45
Lee, Thomas	6	95
Smith, Jeff	6	95
Boyd, Rhoda	7	100
Leininger, Regina	7	50
Korn, Adolph	8	100
McCullough, John	8	95
Gyles, John	9	10
Lehmann, Herman	9	95
Studebaker, Elizabeth	9	100
Lyons, Warren	10	50
McLennan, John	10	85
Slover, John	12	50
Brickell, John	13	40
Tahan	13	100
Hunter, John	15	80
Wells, William	19	50
Waggoner, Peter	20	90
Dragoo	22	50
Parker, Cynthia Ann	24	100
Alder, Jonathan	25	55
Tanner, John	30	60
Brayton, Matthew	34	90
Ward, John	34	100
Armstrong, Robert	38	65
Sage, Caty	61	95
Hoah-Wah	66	95
Long Horn	66	95
Durgan, Millie	70	100
Jemison, Mary	75	65
Moxie	75	95

An analysis of the chart reveals that although captives held for fewer than five years were less assimilated, by and large, than those held for longer periods, there were many who became highly Indianized in a half decade or less. It is notable, also, that several captives who lived with the Indians for more than twenty years became less assimilated than others held for comparatively brief periods. Clearly, then, length of captivity was not the most crucial factor in assimilation.

Notes

1. Walter Prescott Webb, The Texas Rangers. (Austin, 1965), 35-38.

2. Rister, Border Captives, 133-34.

3. J. Marvin Hunter, Horrors of Indian Captivity. (Bandera, Tex., 1937), 70-77.

4. Charles F. Lummis, General Crook and the Apache Wars. (Flagstaff, Arizona, 1966), 45-46.

5. T. A. Babb, In the Bosom of the Comanches. (Amarillo, 1923), 19-64.

6. F. M. Buckalew, Buckalew, the Indian Captive. (Mason, Tex., 1911), 19-26, 44-47, 73, 96-104.

7. Pierre Esprit Radisson, Voyages. (New York, 1943), 1-85.

8. Corwin, Comanche & Kiowa Captives, 178-83.

9. George W. Hill, "The Captivity of Christian Fast," in W. W. Beach, The Indian Miscellany. (Albany, 1877), 51-64.

Chapter 8

THE CRITICAL AGE

It becomes increasingly apparent when analyzing narratives of captivity that the age when captured was the crucial factor which determined the degree of assimilation. This chapter considers the histories of a number of youthful captives in an attempt to establish whether there was a critical age which determined the individual's inclination to remain with the Indians or to return to his white family if given the opportunity. Further, it attempts to learn whether this critical age was the same for boys and girls. The following case studies are presented in ascending order of age at time of capture:

Captivity of Thomas Armstrong

Thomas Armstrong was captured in Pennsylvania by the Seneca Indians during the American Revolution. He was not more than two years old when taken. After the Iroquois were defeated by an American army they agreed to release all of their captives, but Thomas was one of a considerable number choosing to remain with the Indians. He married a white girl who had been captured in infancy and who was so completely assimilated that an observer described her as "essentially Indian in all save blood."

Many years later, Armstrong lived on a reservation where he frequently came into contact with whites and acquired some use of the English language. He related that "he was so young when taken from his family that he had no recollection of home or kindred, or if any it was so vague and indistinct, as to appear like the shadow of a far off dream...." But it was obvious to him that he was not an Indian and he gradually developed a longing to learn about his life with his white family. The Indians told him where he had been captured and that he had a sister still living near that place. When about twenty years old he went to Pennsylvania and located the home of his sister. Although she did

not recognize him she invited him inside and treated him
kindly.   He made no attempt to speak to her and after about
an hour he returned to the wilderness.   Asked why he had
not made himself known to his sister, he replied that he
"looked like an Indian, and no doubt his sister regarded him
as such ... , that his knowledge of the English language was
so imperfect that he could not have held a conversation with
her, ... and everything looked to him so ... imposing ...
that he was completely overawed, ... thus losing the only
opportunity he ever had of knowing and becoming known to the
only person living ... allied to him by ties of consanguin-
ity."[1]

Captivity of John Ward

Another captive who lived with the Indians until his
death was John Ward.   Captured in 1758 at the age of three
by Shawnee Indians, he was completely assimilated, married
an Indian, and fathered several children.   He had the unusual
experience of fighting against members of his own white
family on at least three separate occasions.   As a young
warrior he fought in a battle near the mouth of the Kanawha
River in which his white father was killed.   His half-Indian
daughter was almost killed by a white brother in a surprise
attack on the Shawnee village in 1791.   A year later his
brother, James Ward, was a member of the Kentucky militia
which attacked his village.   John Ward was mortally wounded
and James could hear him groaning and calling for help in
the Shawnee language.   He had lived with the Indians thirty-
four years at the time he was killed. [2]

Captivity of Robert Armstrong

Robert Armstrong was captured by Wyandot Indians
near Pittsburgh, Pennsylvania, in 1786.   He was approximately four years old at the time.   Adopted into the Big
Turtle band, he became an expert hunter and married an Indian.   A missionary who saw him said that he "had become
a perfect Indian in his feelings and habits of life; and had so
far lost the knowledge of his mother tongue that he could
speak and understand but little of it. "

So far as is known Robert and Thomas Armstrong were not related but both of them made some rap-
prochement toward white civilization after being placed on

reservations. Robert eventually regained a sufficient knowledge of English to serve the missionaries as an interpreter.
He became a Christian and attempted to convert the Wyandots
to that faith. His second wife was half white, the daughter
of a famous captive named Isaac Zane. [3]

Captivity of White Chief

A child who was captured at the age of four and became a chief of the Iroquois gave an account of his experiences to missionaries many years later. He did not remember his family name and was known only as White Chief.
"The last I remember of my mother, she was running, carrying me in her arms," he related. "Suddenly she fell to the
ground ... and I was taken from her. Overwhelmed with
fright, I knew nothing more until I opened my eyes to find
myself in the lap of an Indian woman. Looking kindly down
into my face she smiled on me, and gave me some dried
deer's meat and maple sugar. From that hour I believe she
loved me as a mother. I am sure I returned to her the affection of a son.... I always had a warm place at the fire,
and slept in her arms...."

After a few years of captivity the boy became more
adept than his companions at racing and other Indian contests.
Angered by his superiority, the young Indians taunted him
with being white. "I immediately hung my head and ran ...
to my mother, and ... cried bitterly and loudly," he recalled. "She soothed me as well as she could, asking what
was the matter. After a while I was able to tell her the
bitter taunt I had received. She took me in her arms and
said, 'Well, my son it is true. You are a white boy. You
can't help it; but if you always do right and are smart, you
will be none the worse for belonging to that wicked race.'"

When he matured he took the warpath against enemy
tribes but never did fight against the whites. He became a
chief at an early age and married an Indian maiden. They
had three sons, all of whom eventually became chiefs. Once
again some of the Indians were envious and for a time he
considered leaving them to live with the whites. But his Indian relatives prevailed on him to remain and he told the
missionaries that he never regretted his decision to live out
his days with the tribe. [4]

Captivity of Caty Sage

Caty Sage was kidnapped at the age of five in Elk Creek Valley, Virginia, in 1792. She grew up with the Wyandot Indians and lived with them until her death sixty-one years later. She survived three Indian husbands, two of whom, the Crain and Between-the-Logs, were important chiefs.

In 1848 her brother, Charles, located her in Kansas after the Wyandots had been removed to that place. She could neither, speak nor understand English and she declined to return to Virginia to visit her relatives. She told her brother to write her aged mother the following message: "Though you may think my lot has been a hard one--and certainly it has--I have no reason to complain. I have always been treated tenderly in the way I have been raised."[5]

Captivity of Jacob Nicely

Jacob Nicely was captured at the age of five by Seneca Indians in Westmoreland County, Pennsylvania. Nothing was known of him for almost forty years. Finally, in 1828 his family learned that he was living on the Seneca Reservation. Jacob's brother visited him and found that he had acquired an Indian wife and a considerable amount of property and was well satisfied with the Indian way of life.

Jacob's brother urged him to make a visit to his aged mother in Pennsylvania, and finally he agreed to do so. The brothers rode south on horseback but they had not gone far when Jacob changed his mind. He promised to make the trip the following summer but he never left the Indians again.[6]

Captivity of Thomas Lee

Thomas Lee was taken during a foray into Union County, Pennsylvania, on August 13, 1782. He was about six years old at the time. His father and mother were killed in the raid. His baby brother was bashed against a tree and left for dead but survived the blow and was rescued by neighbors.

Thomas lived with the Indians until he was ransomed by relatives in 1788. He became so attached to his adopted family that it was necessary to bind him in the canoe on the

way back to Pennsylvania.   When the party reached Wilkes-
Barre they untied the youth and he immediately leaped from
the canoe and fled into the woods.   After several hours of
searching, Thomas was located and closely guarded during
the remainder of the trip.   After reaching home he was sullen
and longed to return to the Indians, but gradually became
reaccustomed to white civilization. [7]

Captivity of Silas and Timothy Rice

Silas Rice, 9, and his brother Timothy, 7, were captured by Iroquois Indians in 1704.   Taken to an Indian village
on the St. Lawrence, they were adopted into the families of
chiefs as replacements for sons killed in battle.   As the boys
grew into young manhood they lost the use of English and
married Indians.   They adopted the ways of their captors and
in time exhibited such qualities of leadership that they became
the most prominent chiefs among the remnant of the Six Nations at Cauhnawaga.

In 1749 a relative of the Rices found Timothy and in-
duced him to visit his original home.   He remembered the
site and the events of his capture but he had no desire to
abandon his Indian family.

Timothy lived until 1777 and Silas until 1779.   They
left almost seven hundred descendants, many of whom became
Iroquois leaders. [8]

Captivity of Kiowa Dutch

In 1837 the Kiowas raided the Matagorda Bay area of
Texas and massacred a German family.   They spared an
eight-year-old boy and carried him into captivity.   He remained with them for sixty years.   The boy grew into a fear-
some warrior, known throughout the Texas frontier as Kiowa
Dutch.   An enormous blond, no amount of exposure to the
sun could make him resemble his Indian companions, but culturally he was as much a Kiowa as if he had been born into
the tribe.

In August 1866 an Army wagon train was attacked by
the band of the famous raider, Satanta, near the Llano River
in Central Texas.   A severe fight lasted most of the day.
Finally the Indians broke off the engagement, but before they

left the scene Kiowa Dutch rode close enough to the wagons
to curse the soldiers in English, spoken with a German ac-
cent.   He warned them that he would get their scalps before
they reached Buffalo Gap.

In 1890 the Kiowas were living peacefully on the reservation in Oklahoma.   There an Indian agent interviewed
Kiowa Dutch.   The captive recalled attending school in Germany for one year and then moving with his family to Texas
where they settled on a river near the sea.   After the Indians
killed his family he had never felt any desire to return to
white civilization.   He could not recall his family name. [9]

Captivity of Jonathan Alder

Jonathan Alder, aged 9, was captured by Shawnee Indians in Wythe County, Virginia, in March 1782.   A chief
named Succohanos adopted him as a replacement for a son who
had died.   Jonathan's adopted parents tried in every possible
way to make him happy, but for a long time he cried to return to his white family.   After he learned their language he
became satisfied with his new life and would have been perfectly content had it not been for repeated attacks of fever
and ague.

In a short time Alder became an expert hunter and
when he was only thirteen years old he went on his first horse
stealing raid into Kentucky.   Ten years later he encountered
some white settlers who reported that he had almost completely lost the use of the English language.

After General Anthony Wayne's victory brought peace
to the area, Alder and his Indian wife built a cabin near a
white settlement.   Gradually he began to lose his love of the
Indian way of life and to desire to locate his white relatives.
A white neighbor advertised for him in the newspapers and
as a result he was reunited with his brother.   Alder then
separated from his Indian wife, giving her all his property,
and went home to Virginia to live as a white man. [10]

Captivity of Cynthia Ann Parker

On May 19, 1836, a war party of eight hundred Comanches, Kiowas, and Wichitas struck at Parker's Fort in
east central Texas, killing five men and taking four captives:

Cynthia Ann Parker (aged nine); her younger brother, John; her aunt, Mrs. Rachel Plummer; and Mrs. Plummer's fifteen-month-old son, Jimmy.

Mrs. Plummer was redeemed in 1838. She wrote a starkly moving narrative of the loss of her son, Jimmy, who was taken from her, and of the murder of an infant to whom she gave birth five months after her capture. Her ordeals had wrecked her health. She was ill when redeemed and died the following year. John Parker and little Jimmy Plummer were ransomed by General Zachary Taylor in 1842. After six years of captivity neither of them could speak English and both were afraid of white people.

In 1846, an Army officer saw Cynthia Ann and tried unsuccessfully to purchase her. By this time she had become completely Indianized and probably was married. [11] Six years later, Captain Randolph B. Marcy, who was exploring the Red River for the U. S. Government, reported as follows:

> This woman has adopted all the habits and peculiarities of the Comanches; has an Indian husband (Peta Nocona, a war chief) and children, and cannot be persuaded to leave them. The brother (John Parker) of the woman ... was sent back by his mother for the purpose of endeavoring to prevail upon his sister to leave the Indians, and return to her family; but he stated to me that on his arrival she refused to listen to the proposition, saying that her husband, children, and all that she held most dear, were with the Indians, and there she should remain. [12]

In 1860, Cynthia Ann was recovered by Texas Ranger Captain L. S. Ross during a surprise attack on a Comanche camp. With her was an infant daughter. Ross sent word to her uncle, Isaac Parker. After attempting to converse with her, Parker finally concluded that she was not Cynthia Ann. But the name had a familiar sound to the long-lost captive. She pointed to herself and repeated "Cynthia Ann." She left two sons among the Comanches, one of whom became the famous war chief known as Quanah Parker. [13]

Captivity of Samuel Gill

Samuel Gill, son of Sergeant Samuel Gill of Salisbury,

Massachusetts, was almost ten years old when captured by
Abenaki Indians on June 10, 1697. He was taken to Canada
and lived with the Indians the rest of his life. About 1715
he married a white captive named Rosalie (not otherwise
identified since the record was destroyed by Major Robert
Rogers in his raid against the tribe during the French and
Indian War.) They lived like Indians, but Samuel never lost
the use of the English language.

Samuel and Rosalie had several children, most of whom
married Indians. Their sons became important members of
the Abenaki tribe. In 1768 their descendants made an attempt
to locate their relatives in New England. Their memorandum
was worded as follows:

> We ... have come together to choose one among us
> to seek the relatives of our late father, a native of
> New England. We have never known exactly where
> he was taken, only that he was brought 80 years
> ago to St. Francis. His name was Same Gille, We
> know also that our grandfather, Sagen Gill, sent
> twice to seek him, but he, having been taken so
> young, had become attached to the nation and never
> wished to leave.... [14]

Captivity of John Tarbell

John Tarbell was born in July 1695. He was almost
twelve years old when captured at Groton, N.H., and taken
to Canada, along with an older sister, Sarah, and a seven-
year-old brother, Zechariah. Sarah was bought by the French
and the boys remained with the Indians.

John and Zechariah lived at the Indian towns of Caug-
nawago and St. Regis. They did not forget their New England
family, however, and in 1739 they visited Groton. Many
citizens, including the Governor, attempted to induce them to
remain, offering money and land, but they were determined
to return to their Indian families.

Thomas Hutchinson, Colonial official and historian,
wrote that "I met at Albany two or three men in 1744, who
came in with the Indians to trade, and who had been taken at
Groton ... one of them ------- Tarbell was said to be one
of the wealthiest of the Cagnawaga tribe. He made a visit in
his Indian dress and with his Indian complexion (for by means

of grease and paints but little difference could be discerned)
to his relatives at Groton but had no inclination to remain
there. "[15]

Captivity of John Longley

John Longley was born in 1682 and captured at Groton
when he was twelve years old. His father and mother and
five brothers and sisters were killed by the Indians and he
and two younger sisters were carried to Canada. Both sisters died in Canada, one after many years as a nun. John
was redeemed after four years of captivity. He was ransomed against his will and had to be tied on the trip home
to keep him from rejoining the Indians. [16]

Captivity of Warren Lyons

Warren Lyons was captured in 1837 by Comanches in
Lavaca County, Texas. He was thirteen years old when
taken and he remained with the Indians ten years. He had
several opportunities to escape but, knowing that the Indians
had killed his father and suspecting that his mother had left
the area, he believed that he had no home to return to. In
1847 he accompanied the Comanches into San Antonio to trade.
There he was recognized by friends of the family who told
him his mother still lived in Lavaca County and urged him to
return home. Warren, who still retained the use of English,
protested that he had two young Indian wives and did not wish
to leave them. He was given a large number of presents as
an inducement to visit his mother but he remained obdurate
until his consent was obtained by the gift of two beautiful
blankets, one for each wife. Then he promised only to make
a brief visit and insisted that he would return to his Indian
wives and friends. He had every intention of rejoining the
Indians but finally was persuaded to join the Texas Rangers
by a brother who belonged to that organization. [17]

Captivity of the Girty Brothers

The importance of age at the time of capture in determining the course of assimilation is clearly demonstrated
when studying the cases of siblings. One of the most interesting captivities of this kind was that of Simon Girty, the
infamous "white savage, " who terrorized Kentucky from 1778

to 1794.   Girty was taken along with his mother, stepfather,
three brothers, and a stepbrother at the fall of Fort Gran-
ville, Pennsylvania, in 1756.

John Turner, the stepfather, was tortured to death
while the family was forced to watch.   Mrs. Turner and her
small son, John, were taken by the Delawares and remained
with them until they were released in 1759.   The four Girty
boys--Thomas, Simon, James, and George--were held at
Kittanning.   Only a few weeks after their arrival there the
town was attacked by Col. John Armstrong.   Thomas, the
oldest brother, was redeemed.   Simon, aged fifteen, was
held by the Senecas; James, aged thirteen, by the Shawnees;
and George, aged eleven, by the Delawares.   Each of them
remained with the Indians three years, being released in 1759
along with their mother and stepbrother.

During the American Revolution the three younger
Girty brothers were employed in the British Indian service
and participated in many raids against the Kentucky settlements.   Simon became so notorious for acts of cruelty and
treachery that his very name struck terror throughout the
frontier.   It was commonly believed that he had become a
complete Indian, more dangerous than the warriors he led.
But Consul W. Butterfield, biographer of the Girtys, contends
that Simon was not thoroughly Indianized: "Girty was at
times ... ferociously cruel, and exhibited the utmost savagery, but he was not at heart an Indian; nor did he leave
Pittsburgh to throw in his lot with 'the dusky companions of
his forest life, ' but with 'their allies, ' the British. "

In 1784 Simon married Catherine Malott, a captive
who had been held by the Delawares since 1780.   He secured
her release from captivity and they built a cabin in Canada
near Detroit.   Although Simon spent much of his time with
Indians, he and his wife lived as whites.

James Girty married a Shawnee and became more Indianized then his older brother.   Although less notorious than
Simon, he, also, has been characterized as a complete
savage.   But Butterfield contends otherwise: "He had a cruel
and savage nature, it is true, but he had by no means given
himself up to the ... life of an Indian, living upon scanty
food like the red men, hunting as they did, dressing like
them, or depending upon gifts from the British, or obtaining
the necessaries of life by selling skins to the traders.   He
was himself a trader, and a thrifty one.... "

The youngest Girty brother, George, like Simon and James, participated in many raids against the settlements. But unlike his brothers he eventually reverted to the Indian life style, married a Delaware, and fathered several children. He is said to have attempted whenever possible to influence white captives to accept the Indian way of life. [18]

Captivity of Joanna Ordway

Joanna Ordway was captured in Massachusetts in 1704. She was 17 to 19 years old. For several years she roamed the woods with the Abenakis and was with them during a fight with white men. In the spring of 1707 a party of Deerfield scouts encountered some Abenakis near Lake Champlain and wounded one of them. A scout rushed forward to obtain a scalp and was startled to see that the intended victim was a white woman who scrambled away into the wilderness. From his description she was thought to be Joanna Ordway.

On June 22, 1710, a French priest baptized Joanna's Indian baby girl, "born six months ago in the woods, that an English girl, named Jeanne Owardway, taken at Haverhill in New England in the winter of 1704 by the Abenakis of the river of Bequancour, has had by an Abenaki savage. "

The baby was named Marguerite Abenaki. Joanna was unable to sign the certificate. Apparently she was sold to the French, for she was living in Montreal in 1713. [19]

Captivity of James Smith

James Smith was eighteen years old when captured by Canafatauga and Delaware Indians while on a road-cutting expedition near Fort Loudoun, Pennsylvania, in May 1755. He was taken to Fort Duquesne and forced to run the gauntlet, but his life was spared while many other captives were burned.

A few days later he was taken to a large Indian town on the Muskingum River. Expecting a fiery death, he was, instead, adopted by an Indian family. After his redemption he wrote a valuable account of his experiences:

> At length one of the chiefs made a speech.... 'My son, you are now flesh of our flesh, and bone of

our bone. By the ceremony which was performed
this day, every drop of white blood was washed
from your veins; you are taken into the Caughnewago
nation, and initiated into a warlike tribe; you are
adopted into a great family.... My son, you have
nothing to fear, we are now under the same obliga-
tions to love, support, and defend you, that we are
to love and defend one another, therefore you are
to consider yourself one of our people. ' --- At
this time I did not believe this fine speech, especially that of the white blood being washed out of
me; but since that time I have found that there was
much sincerity in said speech--for from that day I
never knew them to make any distinction between
me and themselves in any respect whatever until I
left them. --- If they had plenty of clothing I had
plenty, if we were scarce we all shared the same
fate.

Smith went on hunting trips with the Indians almost
from the day of his adoption and he quickly learned their
language. His band raided the settlements many times but
he was not taken along. "Though they had been exceeding
kind to me, I still detested them, on account of the barbarity
I beheld after Braddock's defeat. ... but I began now to excuse the Indians on account of their want of information, " he
wrote.

During the winter of 1757-58, Smith was living with
an elderly and crippled adopted Indian brother and a little
boy. They were at the point of starvation. He decided to
try to escape to the nearest settlements. After traveling
about twelve miles he saw buffalo tracks and followed them
until he made a kill. "When hunger was abated, I began to
be tenderly concerned for my old Indian brother, and the
little boy I had left in a perishing condition, " he recalled.
"I made haste and packed up what meat I could carry ... and
returned homewards. "

Home in this case meant his Indian family. Smith
remained with the Indians for another year and a half. Then
he accompanied some Indians to Montreal where he managed
to get aboard a French ship carrying English prisoners to be
exchanged. He reached home in 1760. [20]

Conclusions

The foregoing narratives indicate that the critical age for Indianization was about twelve years. Most children taken below that age were easily assimilated. Those older than twelve accepted many of the ways of the Indians but, in most cases, retained the desire to return to their white families. In order to test this thesis, a chart has been prepared to evaluate the assimilation status of approximately fifty captives, aged eighteen and under. Factors considered in determining the degree of assimilation include knowledge of Indian languages, acquiring skill in Indian activities, attempts to escape, attachment to individual Indians, participation in warfare against other tribes, raids against whites, Indian marriages, and acceptance or rejection of opportunities to return to white families.

Name of Captive	Age of Captivity	Degree of Assimilation
Armstrong, Thomas	1	90%
Doddridge (girl)	2	95
White Chief	4	95
Moxie, John Valentine	5	90
Hunter, John Dunn	5	80
Saenz, Bernardino	5	100
Slocum, Frances	5	90
Tahan (Texas Man)	5	100
French, Abigail	6	100
Smith, Jeff	6	95
Brayton, Matthew	7	90
Williams, Eunice	7	70
Hoah-Wah (boy)	7	95
Stone (boy)	7	70
Kellogg, Rebecca	8	80
Brown, Adam	8	90
Slover, John	8	50
Korn, Adolph	8	100
Hurst, Hannah	8	100
M'Cullough, John	8	95
Waggoner, Peter	8	90
Long Horn (boy)	9	95
Parker, Cynthia Ann	9	100
Gill, Samuel	9	60
Harris, Mary	9	80
Searls, Elisha	9	60

Name of Captive	Age of Captivity	Degree of Assimilation
Tanner, John	9	60 %
Zane, Isaac	9	75
Malone, Rachel	10	75
Carter, Mercy	10	65
Girty, George	11	60
Kellogg, Joanna	11	60
Lehmann, Herman	11	95
Smith, Clinton	11	90
Tarbell, John	11	80
Jemison, Mary	12	65
Leininger, Barbara	12	20
Le Roy, Marie	12	20
Oatman, Olive	12	15
Longley, John	12	60
Babb, T. A.	13	45
Lyons, Warren	13	50
Girty, James	13	50
Boyd, Thomas	13	55
Boyeau, Mary	14	10
Gibson, Hugh	14	15
Girty, Simon	15	40
Schoolcraft, Leonard	16	100
Diaz, Martina	16	5
Radisson, Pierre Esprit	16	45
Ordway, Joanna	17	50
Smith, James	18	20

Attempting to pinpoint a critical age which separated captives who became Indianized from others who resisted assimilation is difficult because of the imprecise evidence which is available. It is obvious from the foregoing list that many of the captives did not remember their own names. It appears highly unlikely that they would recall their ages at the times they were captured. In many cases, however, the exact date of the capture was known to relatives who recorded it or, perhaps, told it to the captives when they were redeemed. In other instances, painstaking research by such scholars as Emma Lewis Coleman verified ages of captives through court or church records.

A further complicating factor enters the picture when accessing the assimilation of children taken to Canada. Most

of these young captives were sold to the French and became
transformed into French-Canadian Catholics rather than Indians.   For purposes of this study only those New England
children who remained several years in Indian hands are
included.

There are a few captives on the list who appear to
deviate significantly from the age-assimilation pattern.   Joanna Ordway was at least seventeen, possibly nineteen, when
captured by Abenakis.   She roamed the woods with her captor
and had a child by him.   If the Deerfield scouts correctly
identified her she could have been redeemed by them if she
had not run away.   Apparently she never saw her white family again, but evidence exists that she left the Indians to live
in Montreal.   If more were known of the pressures to which
she was subjected, perhaps it would be learned that she was
no more completely assimilated than were other girls her
age.

The captive who deviated most from the age-assimilation pattern was Leonard Schoolcraft.   Taken at sixteen, he
showed the qualities the Indians sought in a potential warrior
when, instead of dodging his assailants while running the
gauntlet, he attacked them with his fists.   "This was the last
certain information which was ever had concerning him, "
stated the reliable antiquarian, Alexander Scott Withers.   But
Schoolcraft was accused of becoming a complete savage and
a threat to his own people.

Nine years after his capture, a war party struck the
settlement of Hacker's Creek.   Withers included an account
of the raid in his Chronicles of Border Warfare which described the deeds of a white man believed to have been
Schoolcraft:

> They then went to the house of Edmund West, Jun.
> where were Mrs. West and her sister (a girl of
> eleven years old, daughter of John Hacker) and a
> lad of twelve, a brother of West.   Forcing open
> the door, Schoolcraft and two of the savages en-
> tered; and one of them immediately tomahawked
> Mrs. West.   The boy was taking some corn from
> under the bed, --he was drawn out by the feet and
> the tomahawk sank twice in his forehead, directly
> above each eye.   The girl was standing behind the
> door.   One of the savages approached and aimed
> at her a blow.   She tried to evade it; but it struck

on the side of her neck, though not with sufficient
force to knock her down.   She fell, however, and
lay as if killed.   Thinking their work of death accomplished here, they took from a press some
milk, butter and bread, placed it on the table, and
deliberately sat down to eat, --the little girl observ-
ing all that passed, in silent stillness.   When they
had satisfied their hunger, they arose, scalped the
woman and boy, plundered the house ... and departed, dragging the little girl by the hair, forty
or fifty yards from the house.   They then threw
her over the fence, and scalped her; but as she
evinced symptoms of life, Schoolcraft observed 'that
is not enough, ' when immediately one of the savages
thrust a knife into her side,' and they left her.
Fortunately the point of the knife came in contact
with a rib and did not injure her much.... [21]

Was Schoolcraft by nature more savagely inclined than
other captives taken at his age?   Or was the renegade really
some other captive who had been with the Indians since early
childhood?   Probably the answers will never be known.

Fortunately, we do have additional information about
the attitudes of a captive who appears to have been less completely assimilated than others taken at his age.   He was
John Slover, captured at the age of eight by the Miamis and
held for twelve years.   In 1773 he was brought to Pittsburgh
by some Shawnee Indians and some of his relatives recognized him and urged him to return home with them.   He
yielded reluctantly, having become strongly attached to the
Indians and their way of life.

During the American Revolution an army under the
command of Col. William Crawford invaded the Indian country
and pressed Slover into service as a guide.   He accepted the
assignment with great reluctance.   The Shawnees and Delawares defeated Crawford's forces and Slover found himself a
prisoner once more.   The Indians upbraided him for turning
against his brothers and, urged on by James Girty, they
threatened to burn him at the stake.

Slover knew many of the chiefs, spoke their language
fluently, and defended himself ably in the council called to
decide his fate.   He reminded them that during the whole
twelve years of his former captivity he had given ample proof
of his fidelity to the Indians.   Although he had had a thousand

opportunities, he had never once attempted to escape and there were several warriors present who could testify that at the Treaty of Fort Pitt he had left them with reluctance, in compliance with the earnest solicitation of his family. He had then taken leave of them publicly, in broad daylight, in time of peace, and with their full approbation. He then had had no idea he would ever be called upon to oppose them in a future war, but when war broke out it was his duty to accompany his countrymen to the field against the Indians, precisely as he would have accompanied the Indians against the whites if he had remained with them. In conclusion he stated that "it was the undoubted duty of every warrior to serve his country, without regard to his own private feelings of attachment; that he had done so; and if the Indians thought it worthy of death, they could inflict the penalty upon him!"

The decision of the Indian council was to burn the captive. They fastened Slover to the stake and set fire to the faggots. But suddenly a downpour of rain extinguished the fire. His torture was then reset for the next day. During the night his guards fell asleep and he loosened his bonds and escaped into the darkness. Several days later he reached safety at Wheeling. [22]

These cases notwithstanding, it is believed that a pattern of assimilation, based upon age at time of capture, is discernible from the chart. With few exceptions, children captured below the age of twelve became greatly Indianized. With few exceptions, teen-aged female captives, although they accepted many features of Indian life, retained the desire to return to white civilization. It appears, therefore, that the age of twelve can be considered the dividing line between female captives who preferred to remain with Indians and those who sought to return to their white families. Evidence is strong that male captives taken during their early teens were attracted to many phases of Indian life, and the critical age appears to have approximated fourteen. It is perhaps notable that for both boys and girls these critical periods coincide with the commonly designated ages of puberty.

Notes

1.   Orlando Allen, "Incidents in the Life of an Indian Captive," in American Historical Record, I (1872), 409-10.

2.   Charles McKnight, Our Western Border. (Philadelphia,
     1879), 598-603.

3.   James B. Finley, Life Among the Indians. (Cincinnati,
     n. d.), 455-56.

4.   Harriet S. Caswell, Our Life Among the Iroquois In-
     dians. (Boston, 1892), 53-55.

5.   Bonnie Sage Ball, Red Trails and White. (N. Y. 1955),
     19-20, 37-38, 40-41, 51, 58, 61-62.

6.   Sipe, The Indian Wars of Pennsylvania, 696.

7.   Ibid, 675-76.

8.   Edward P. Spillane, "An Iroquois Chief, " United States
     Catholic Historical Society Historical Records and
     Studies, VI, Part 1 (February 1911), 103-04.

9.   Wharton, Satanta, 14, 59.

10. Charles McKnight, Our Western Border. (Philadelphia,
     1879), 602-03, 728-31.

11. Peckham, Captured by Indians, 184-192.

12. Randolph B. Marcy, Exploration of the Red River of
     Louisiana in the Year 1852. (Washington, 1854), 103.

13. Peckham, Captured by Indians, 192-94.

14. Coleman, New England Captives Carried to Canada, II,
     360-64.

15. Ibid, I, 293-97.

16. Ibid, I, 284-85.

17. James T. DeShields, The Border Wars of Texas.
     (Tioga, Tex. , 1912), 229-31.

18. Consul Willshire Butterfield, History of the Girtys.
     (Columbus, 1950), 56, 232, 293-94, 315.

19. Coleman, New England Captives Carried to Canada, I,
     350-52.

20. James Smith, <u>An Account of the Remarkable Occur-
     rences in the Life and Travels of Col. James Smith.</u>
     (Cincinnati, 1907).

21. Withers, <u>Chronicles of Border Warfare,</u> 377-80.

22. John A. M'Clung, <u>Sketches of Western Adventure.</u> (Cov-
     ington, Ky. , 1872), 145-57.

Chapter 9

REDEEMED CAPTIVES:
THEIR STRUGGLE TO READJUST

The number of captives living out their lives with Indians was probably considerably smaller than the number restored to their white families. While it would seem that
restoration would result in rapid reacculturation for all save
those captured at a very early age, there is evidence that for
many former captives the readjustment to white civilization
was exceedingly difficult. Some redeemed captives died without ever losing the desire to return to the Indians. For
others the transformation required a long period of time and
great patience on the part of their relatives. In some cases
the former captives were able to ease the adjustment by en-
gaging in employment, such as interpreting or trading, which
allowed them to work with Indians. In other instances, male
ex-captives were enticed into giving up the wild, free life of
the Indians only by diverting them into dangerous careers in
the wilderness or on the plains. Thus Nick Wilson became a
Pony Express rider, while others were employed as scouts
and rangers. This chapter presents case studies which illustrate variations in patterns of reassimilation.

Captivity of Elizabeth Studebaker

Elizabeth Studebaker, a small child, was captured in
Cumberland County, Pennsylvania, in 1775. While living with
the Indians she developed into a beautiful maiden who became
a great favorite of her captors. After nine years of captivity
she was among the 206 prisoners delivered up to Colonel
Bouquet near the Muskingum River following his successful
campaign against the Delawares and Shawnees. The former
captives were taken to Fort Pitt and along the route it was
necessary to watch many of them closely to prevent their
running away to rejoin the Indians. One of the most determined to escape from what she considered a "captivity" was
Elizabeth Studebaker. Ten days after the march began she
slipped away into the wilderness to rejoin her adopted people,

the Delawares. [1]

Captivity of Elizabeth Hawkins

Elizabeth Hawkins was captured during early childhood in September 1781 in Washington County, Pennsylvania. She lived most of her life in a Shawnee village north of the Ohio. She became thoroughly assimilated and married a warrior. Restored to her white family when the Indian wars ended in the Old Northwest in 1795, she was never able to rebridge the gap between civilizations. After a short stay among the familiar scenes of her childhood she returned to her Indian husband and was never seen again by her white relatives. [2]

Captivity of the Benjamin Children

In the autumn of 1777, Indians attacked the Benjamin family of Lycoming County, Pennsylvania, killing the parents and capturing the children--William, Nathan, Ezekiel, and their little sister. The boys were restored after the Revolution ended but the girl remained among the Indians, married a warrior, and bore him several children. In later years William located his sister and brought her to his home in Williamsport. There she remained for a brief time, miserable and longing for her Indian companions. Finally, William relented and permitted her to return to her home in the wilderness. [3]

Restoration of Cynthia Ann Parker

Cynthia Ann Parker, whose captivity by Comanches was described in the preceding chapter, was redeemed by Captain Sul Ross on December 18, 1860. With her was an eighteen-old daughter, Topsannah (Prairie Flower), whose father was Chief Peta Nacona. Mildred P. Mayhall, in her interesting book, The Indian Wars of Texas, stated that Cynthia Ann had loved her Indian family deeply and was one of the many captives who "entered the life of the tribe with zest" and "grew to love the free life, even preferred it to the hum-drum existence of civilized communities."

Thirty-four years old at the time of her redemption, Cynthia Ann was taken to live at the home of an uncle. Gradually she regained the use of English and became a success-

ful housekeeper but she was always bitter and miserable.
Several times she tried to escape, only to have relatives
catch up with her. She was so anxious about the fate of her
half-Indian sons that she scarified her chest, put the blood
on tobacco and burned it, wailing to the spirits to preserve
the lives of her children. Civilization seemed not to agree
with little Topsannah, who soon sickened and died. After
this loss, Cynthia Ann was so broken in spirit that she lit-
erally starved herself to death. [4]

Restoration of Lizzie Ross

        Captain Sul Ross, the Ranger who reclaimed Cynthia
Ann Parker, was the central figure in redeeming another white
captive, this time with quite different results. In September
1858, during a battle near the present Rush Springs, Oklahoma, he saw a white girl among the Comanches and seized
her as she was fleeing. The girl, about eight years old, was
terrified at finding herself a "captive" of the whites. She
didn't recall any life but that of the Indians, and her identity
was never discovered. Ross adopted her, naming her Lizzie
after his fiancee. He saw to it that she obtained a good education and she lived with his family while he attained high
political office, including the governorship of Texas. Apparently she experienced little difficulty in returning to a civilization which she could not even remember. In 1889 she
married a wealthy California merchant. [5]

Restoration of Warren Lyons

        The preceding chapter included a section on the cap-
tivity of Warren Lyons. He had been home but a few days
when he began to miss his Indian friends. All of his relatives and neighbors conspired to detain him, but he was fully
resolved to rejoin the Indians until his brother, a Texas
Ranger, persuaded him to sign up with the organization.
James T. DeShields noted in his Border Wars of Texas that
"this service gradually weaned him from his Indian habits,
and reconciled him to civilization, ending in his marriage and
domestic life; not, however, till he had participated in several engagements with the Indians, in which, like his brothers,
he developed the characteristics of a courageous soldier. "[6]

Captivity and Restoration of Dan M'Allum

Dan M'Allum was captured at the age of two by Mohawk Indians soon after the beginning of the American Revolution.   When the war ended, the Indians were compelled to give up their captives but Dan tried desperately to rejoin his beloved Mohawk mother.   George Peck, a neighbor of the boy's parents, described Dan's difficulties in readjusting to white civilization:

> And now another trial awaited the poor boy.   The usages of civilization were like the chains of slavery to him.   To wear pants and jacket, and sleep upon a bed, and to eat bread ... all this was so strange--everything so unnatural....
>
> 'Dan M'Allum, ' so long as we knew him, which was until we entered our eightieth year, exhibited strong traits of Indian character.   He was fond of hunting, loved rum, would have his Indian pow-wows, and, when under the influence of the intoxicating draught, his Indian whoop rang through the neighborhood....
> Often have we heard the poor fellow say, apparently from the bottom of his heart, 'I wish to God I had never left the Indians, for I was a good Indian, but I shall never make a white man.' He finally married and settled, and his character became much modified by the kindly influences of home....   When he was no longer regarded as 'a fool, ' 'an Indian booby, ' and the like, his manhood developed, and he became a respectable citizen; but the process of transformation was slow and painful.
>
> A curious fact in this case was that the poor Indian captive seemed not to have much affection for his real mother.   He never made a secret of the fact that he loved his 'Indian mother' the best. [7]

Captivity and Restoration of John McLennan

In the spring of 1836, a seven-year-old Texas boy named John McLennan was captured by Waco Indians.   His parents were killed in the raid and two younger brothers soon died in captivity.   John lived with the Indians ten years before a treaty resulted in his release.   He had lost the use of the English language and was "the very picture of a wild

warrior. " It was so difficult for his relatives to reconcile
him to white civilization that he was known as "Indian John"
throughout his life. Eventually he married and became a
farmer, but he never forgot his Indian friends and he frequently visited them, bringing large stores of gifts to his
adopted mother to show his appreciation for her tender care
during his decade of captivity. [8]

Restoration of Herman Lehmann

Herman Lehmann, restored against his will after years
of life as a Comanche warrior, has told a revealing story of
the difficulties of abandoning the attractions of Indian civilization.

> My mother was keeping a hotel in Loyal Valley at
> the time of my return, and had several boarders,
> some traveling men; all of the family and many of
> the people of the community gathered around me.
> Some were laughing, some crying, and all talking.
> I did not like this kind of a demonstration and made
> up my mind that I would go back to Quanah Parker.
> The soldiers told my sister, Mina, how I liked my
> food, so she fixed it as near to my whim as pos-
> sible for a civilized person to do. Everyone did
> all that could be done for me, but I did not like
> any of them. That night I would not sleep in the
> house, although they prepared a nice feather bed
> for me and arranged everything for my comfort. I
> made a pallet of my own blankets out on the
> ground. . . .

> My folks prepared a big feast for me and Mina
> came to invite me to the table. I pretended not to
> hear her, but lay on my pallet. I was homesick
> and was planning then to run away from there.
> Finally she induced me to go to the table, and just
> as I was ready to sit down I saw a fine hog ham
> on the table. I kicked over everything in my reach
> and made for the door, but they stopped me and
> motioned for me to come and eat. I pointed to the
> pork and made them understand that if they would
> remove that I would eat. It was removed and I sat
> down and tried to eat, but the food did not suit me
> and the thought of having to eat with hog-eaters
> choked me. I wanted my meat roasted, and I

didn't care for anything....

I went down on the creek, made a bow and a great
many arrows, and waged war against the hog family.
Whenever a shoat came in sight I would kill him,
no matter to whom he belonged.

I would saddle up my pony and go out hunting.
Somebody gave me a Winchester and my step-father
furnished me with cartridges.   Willie always went
with me to watch me and teach me.   I wanted to
kill calves, but Willie made signs to me that it was
wrong.   I insisted that we take all the horses we
saw, but Willie would not allow that, so I was mad
all of the time; in fact nothing pleased me.

When I met children I would give a yell and draw
my bow on them just to see them run.   That was
all the real enjoyment I had.   I would kill deer,
put them on my pony, ride up to the gate, dis-
mount and leave the horse and deer there.   If anybody wanted the deer they had to go and skin and
clean them, I would not.   Somebody had to stake
my pony, too, for I thought work of that kind was
for the squaws.   I was furious if they failed to
roast me the short ribs or tenderloins, but my
people tried to do everything to please me for several months and I began to learn how to behave.

I would try to run away, but Willie would bring me
back and the women would cry around me.   I did
not like tears.

At last the kindness, tenderness, and gentleness of
my good Christian mother, the affectionate love of
my sisters, and the vigilance of my brothers gradually wove a net of love around me that is as last-
ing as time itself. [9]

Restoration of John Tanner

Difficulties in readjusting to white ways were not
solely the result of the experiences of the captive.   White
distrust and hatred of Indians also played a role in making
readjustment almost impossible for captives who had lived
many years with the Indians.   The experiences of John Tan-

ner provide a classic example, for he spent more than twenty
years trying to gain acceptance in white society.

Tanner had been captured at the age of nine and lived
thirty years among the Ojibways.   He had married an Indian
woman and fathered several children.   Although he had long
since lost the use of his native language and could not even
remember his name, he, like several other captives, developed a desire in later life to learn about his own people
and to return to white civilization.   Noel M. Loomis, in a
valuable introduction to Tanner's narrative, noted that he
"found it--as so many other Indian captives have found it--
impossible.   Though he rejected his Indian foster people and
settled among the whites, educated his halfbreed children in
white schools, still he was too much Indian to change environment.   His Indian characteristics made him 'different. '
He was distrusted by the whites.   He was not prepared or
equipped to make a living according to the white standard.
Confused and bewildered, his white heritage constantly fighting with his acquired Indian environmental factors, in his
later years he was lonely and 'bitter. '

" ... in the early 1840's, in a last desperate attempt
to secure acceptance as a white, he married a white woman
of Detroit.   She bore him one child, but left him because of
what to her were squalor and brutality; eventually she was
granted a divorce by the legislature.   In 1846, perhaps not too
long after his wife left him, he disappeared. ... "[10]

Captivity and Restoration of Isaac Bradley

By no means all restored captives who had been taken
in youth retained an affection for their former captors and
some became inveterate Indian haters.   Probably none of
them exceeded Isaac Bradley in revenging himself upon the
race which had held him in bondage.

Bradley was captured in 1695 by the Abenaki Indians
of Pigwacket.   He was sixteen years old at the time.   For
two years he lived the life of an Indian.   Then one night he
escaped, taking another youth with him.   They fled down the
Seco River and when his companion became exhausted Bradley
carried him on his back to safety.

Bradley had had thirteen members of his family killed
by Indians.   For this he exacted a terrible toll.   He led a

band of scalp hunters on repeated raids against the Abenakis, killing or capturing fifteen Indians, one for each lost relative and for the two years he spent in captivity. [11]

Captivity and Restoration of William Wells

William Wells was captured at the age of 12 in February 1775. He was destined to become a prominent warrior against the whites and, after restoration, a famous leader of scouts against the Indians. Wells grew up with the Miami tribe and married a sister of the famous war chief, Little Turtle. He fought beside Little Turtle in the Indian victories over Generals Harmar and St. Clair, but by the time General Anthony Wayne's army invaded the Indian country he had developed a desire to return to white civilization. According to the reliable antiquarian, Charles McKnight, he parted from the Indians in the following manner:

> Taking with him the great war chief, Little Turtle, to a secluded spot on the Maumee, Wells said to him: 'I now leave your nation for my own people; we have long been friends. We are friends yet until the sun reaches that height (which he indicated). From that time we are enemies. Then if you wish to kill me, you may. If I want to kill you, I may.' At the appointed hour, crossing the river, Wells plunged into the forest and struck the trail of Wayne's army.

Wells proved to be an invaluable asset to General Wayne. He knew the country and understood Indian warfare as did few men of his time. Commissioned captain, he served as the leader of a corps of rangers, many of whom were former captives. Wells and his men killed or captured more than forty warriors, frequently bringing in prisoners who were compelled to divulge the plans of the Indians.

After Wayne's great victory brought peace to the region, Wells went back to the Miami country. But this time he was serving the United States Government in the capacity of Indian agent. His first wife having died, he married another sister of Little Turtle. They lived in the fashion of whites and he had his children educated. [12]

Wells and a band of Miami scouts served the United States when Indian outbreaks occurred during the War of 1812.

Learning that the white people at Fort Dearborn were threatened by Potawatomis, he led fifteen Miamis into Chicago on
August 14, 1812. On the following morning the troops and
white residents evacuated the fort. Wells led the march,
hoping to guard against an ambush. When the Potawatomis
struck the column, Wells led a counter attack and was killed
in the battle which resulted in the Fort Dearborn massacre.[13]

Conclusions

In considering the foregoing cases, as well as others
too numerous for inclusion, no clear-cut pattern emerges.
It is plain that re-acceptance of white civilization was difficult for most and impossible for some redeemed captives.
But others resumed the white way of life almost as if it had
never been interrupted.

While it was possible, to this researcher's satisfaction, to establish age at time of capture as the determining
factor in Indianization, it is impossible to demonstrate con-
clusively that the younger the child when captured by Indians
the more difficult the process of reassimilation when restored to his relatives. Whites taken in their teens experienced little difficulty in readjusting, for few of them had become greatly Indianized. But among captives taken in pre-
adolescence who had become substantially assimilated, it
seems to have mattered little whether they had been captured
as infants or older children. Lizzie Ross, taken too young
to remember any aspect of white civilization, experienced
little difficulty in adjusting to it. Cynthia Ann Parker, captured at the age of nine, found reassimilation impossible.
John Tanner, nine-years-old at time of capture, tried desperately to live as a white man but failed in the end, while
John Hunter, captured in infancy, accomplished the transition
successfully.

Nor is it possible to prove that either length of time
held by the Indians or age at the time of restoration was the
overriding factor in facilitating reacceptance of white culture
patterns. While it is obvious that in most cases a long captivity resulted in a more difficult readjustment, this was by
no means always the case. For Elizabeth Studebaker a
nine-year captivity created too great a gulf to bridge, while
William Wells left the tribe of his own volition after twenty
years of Indian life.

Finally, one wonders how important was the attitude of whites toward the restored captive in easing or retarding readjustment.   Obviously, in the cases of John Tanner and Dan M'Allum hostility and distrust made life difficult.   But in many cases, probably a majority, the redeemed captive was received joyfully and treated with the greatest kindness and consideration.   The narrative of Herman Lehmann and the account of the captivity of Warren Lyons present striking evidence of the determination of relatives to restore the former captives to the white way of life.   In these instances they were successful, but no amount of kindness and patience sufficed to enable Elizabeth Hawkins or the sister of William Benjamin to abandon their Indian characteristics.   Indians they were in every aspect except birth, and Indians they insisted upon remaining for the rest of their lives.   Given a clear choice in the safety of their white families, they must have measured one civilization against the other and found the white way of life wanting in the happiness and fulfillment which they had enjoyed in the lodges of their captors.

Notes

1.   Sipe, Indian Wars of Pennsylvania, 482, 834.

2.   Ibid. , 633-34.

3.   Ibid. , 521.

4.   Mildred P. Mayhall, The Indian Wars of Texas. (Waco, Tex. , 1965), 108-16.

5.   Corwin, Comanche & Kiowa Captives, 117-21.

6.   DeShields, Border Wars of Texas, 230-31.

7.   Peck, The History of Wyoming, 235-37.

8.   DeShields, Border Wars of Texas, 171-72.

9.   Lehmann, Nine Years With the Indians, 205-07.

10.   John Tanner, A Narrative of the Captivity and Adventures of John Tanner.   (Minneapolis, 1956), ix-xiii.

11.   George Hill Evans, Pigwacket, Part I: Old Indian Days in the Valley of the Saco. (Conway, N. H. , 1939), 47-51.

12. McKnight, Our Western Border, 554-61.

13. Mrs. J. H. Kinzie, Wau-Bun. (Chicago, 1901), 172-81.

Chapter 10

INDIAN CHILDREN AND WHITE CIVILIZATION

In the preceding chapter it was pointed out that white captive children, when restored to their original families, found it exceedingly difficult to readjust. It would seem logical to assume that Indian children would find a transition to white civilization even more difficult. This chapter presents case studies of Indian children living among whites and compares their problems of assimilation with those of white children living among Indians.

While there are numerous narratives of captivity of white children raised by Indians, there is little to be found in American frontier annals of Indian children who were captured and reared by whites. Unlike Indians who adopted white children and treated them as their own flesh and blood, the typical frontier family appears to have had little inclination to bring an Indian child into the household. There were a few exceptions, however, as illustrated in the case studies which follow.

Case of Apache May (Patchy Slaughter)

In the spring of 1896 the wealthy Arizona cattleman, John Slaughter, led a troop of cavalry on the trail of a band of Apaches who had jumped the San Carlos Reservation, massacred several settlers, and headed for Mexico. Slaughter located their camp and the soldiers staged a surprise attack. The Indians scattered into the mountains. In their haste they left behind an Apache baby girl, approximately a year old. The baby's father attacked the entire troop in a desperate attempt to regain his child, but the soldiers instantly shot him to death.

John Slaughter decided to raise the child as a member of his own family. Mrs. W. E. Hankin, of Bisbee, Arizona, has written a brief account of the family's experiences:

149

Patchy was just a little wild animal when she came
to San Bernardino Ranch. She ate anything, pick-
ing up scraps of food from the ground. . . .

When she became accustomed to her new home,
she proved an unusually bright child. She understood much that was said to her. Sign language
was natural to her; if she wanted bread and sugar,
her signs were quite eloquent. She was soon lisp-
ing English. She forgot her Indian habits and in a
little while was eating from a plate, drinking from
a cup, and sleeping in her own little bed. . . .

Above everything else in the world, Patchy loved
Mr. Slaughter. She toddled about the place, holding to the strap of one of his boots. . . . If he took
her on his lap, she would sit serenely happy for
any length of time. If he rode away, she would
wait at the gate for hours, watching patiently for
his return.

But Patchy was not always a docile child. When rep-
rimanded by Mrs. Slaughter she became enraged and threatened to kill her adopted mother when she grew up. Neighbors warned the family that the child was incapable of escaping from her savage heritage and that sooner or later she
would present a threat to their safety.

Patchy didn't live long enough to prove or disprove
the theory that heredity would triumph over environment.
Four years after her adoption the child's clothing caught fire
and she burned to death. [1]

Case of Bill Hockley and Maria

In 1840 a detachment of Republic of Texas troops captured two children of a Comanche chief. One, a 14-year-
old boy, was given the name Bill Hockley. The other, an
11-year-old girl, was called Maria. They lived as adopted
children of white families until 1843, when they were returned to the Comanches in an attempt to pacify the power-
ful and warlike tribe. [2] The peace commission, led by
Joseph C. Eldridge and Hamilton P. Bee, located the band
far out on the plains and approached them under a flag of
truce. As Chief Paha-yuca was away on a hunt the commissioners remained in the camp several weeks awaiting his

return.   Fortunately the chief proved to be peaceably inclined,
for he managed after hours of debate to persuade a bare majority of the Comanche council members to respect the flag
of truce.   Before his arrival most of the Indians favored put-
ting the white men to death. [3]

     Maria's return to the Comanches was an ordeal for
her.   She gave no reply to the greetings of her former people
as she could no longer speak a word of Comanche.   Bill
Hockley, too, refused to converse with the Indians during the
absence of their chief, but he remembered the language perfectly well.

     After all other deliberations were concluded Paha-yuca
addressed himself to Bill and Maria.   Bill immediately left
the side of the white commissioners and rejoined his people.
Maria stood mute, holding the hand of Commissioner Eldridge.   When Eldridge attempted to place her hand in the
chief's, she screamed in anguish.   Running behind Eldridge
she begged him

> for God's sake not to give her to those people--to
> have mercy, and not leave her.   Then the poor
> child fell on her knees and shrieked, and clung to
> him with all the madness of despair.   A death-like
> silence prevailed in the council.   The Indians stood
> by in stern stoicism, the voices of the white men
> were silent with emotion, and nothing but the cries
> of the poor lamb of sacrifice pierced the distance
> ...   Her white friends, as soon as possible, at-
> tempted to quiet the child.   Of course the comfort-
> ing words were spoken in their own language, but
> they were evidently understood by all, for their's
> was the language of nature.   Finding their efforts
> useless the chief said:

> 'This is the child of our long mourned chief; she is
> of our blood; her aged grandmother stands ready to
> receive her, but she has forgotten her people.   She
> does not want to come to us, and if the Great White
> Chief only sent her for us to see that she is fat and
> well taken care of, tell him I thank him and she
> can go back. '

> This was an opportunity, and General Bee suggested
> to Colonel Eldridge to save the child; but although
> the latter's heart was bursting with grief and sym-

pathy, his sense of duty told him his work was un-
finished; and he replied to the chief: 'I have been
ordered to give you this child. I have done so, and
my duty is fulfilled. But you see she is no longer
a Comanche; Child in years when she was taken
from you by the stern hand of war, she has learned
the language of another people, and I implore you
to give her to me, and let me take her to my home
and care for her all the days of my life.' 'No,'
said the chief, 'if she is my child I will keep her';
he swung her roughly behind him into the arms of
the old grandmother, who bore her, screaming,
from the council tent, and thus the princess was
delivered to her people; but the last sound the party
heard on leaving the Comanche camp was the wail
of the poor, desolate child. 4

Case of Lydia Carter

Like Patchy, Maria, and Bill Hockley, Lydia Carter
was captured during an Indian war, but her case was quite
different from theirs. She was seized by another Indian tribe
and redeemed by white missionaries.

In October 1817 a large war party of Cherokees,
Shawnees, and Delawares invaded Osage territory, taking
sixty prisoners. Among those captured was an Osage Indian
girl about four years of age whose parents were killed in the
attack. As the Cherokees were returning to their own country
they met a missionary who appealed to them to give him the
child to educate at the Brainerd Indian school. The warrior
who had captured her was noncommital so the missionary
went to Natchez in an attempt to raise funds to offer as ransom. The chief contributor was a Mrs. Lydia Carter, for
whom the child eventually was named. The missionary then
went to Washington and secured the assistance of the Secre-
tary of War, who directed the United States Agent to the
Cherokees to send the child to the Indian school.

Lydia was adopted by the Rev. and Mrs. William
Chamberlain. They taught her to call them father and mother
and treated her as a sister to their own small daughter,
Catherine. Lydia was happy in her new surroundings. She
did well in school and learned the English language in less
than a year.

In 1820 the Osage Indians learned of Lydia's location
and requested her return.   The United States Government
acceded to their demands and sent an agent to the school to
take her back to the tribe.   But Lydia was determined to
stay with her white family.   She fled into the woods and ran
five miles before being overtaken.   She cried and begged to
remain, but to no avail.   On the 900-mile journey back to
the Osage Nation she became ill and died in the home of a
white family. [5]

Experiences of Mary, Daughter of Panisciowa

Mary, an Iroquois Indian girl, was the daughter of
Panisciowa, a warrior who fought under the command of the
Marquis de Lafayette during the American Revolution.   Lafayette wrote a letter of appreciation to Panisciowa which he
gave to Mary at the time of his death.

When Lafayette visited Kaskaskia in 1825, Mary
learned of his presence and called upon him there.   At that
time she told her life story which is of interest for the light
it sheds upon the difficulty experienced by Indians in abandoning the ways of their ancestors.

After the Revolution some of the Iroquois moved to
the Illinois country.   Mary's mother died soon after the move
and Panisciowa took her to visit the United States Indian
Agent at Kaskaskia.   The agent persuaded him to allow the
family to educate Mary along with their own daughter.

Panisciowa promised to return to see her after the
great winter's hunt.   He came, in fact, several times afterwards; and she, notwithstanding the disagreeableness of a
sedentary life, grew up answering the expectations of her
white benefactor and his wife.   She became attached to the
family and readily accepted the Christian religion.   Yet, she
confessed, notwithstanding the influence of religion and civilization, the impressions of her infancy were not entirely
effaced.   If the pleasures of wandering conducted her into the
shady forest she breathed more freely, and it was with reluctance that she returned home.   When, in the cool of the
evening, seated at the door of her adopted father's home, she
heard in the distance the piercing voice of the Indians she
responded with a thrill of joy, imitating the voices, with a
vehemence which frightened the young white girl.   And when
occasionally some warriors came to consult the agent in

regard to their treaties, or hunters to offer him a part of the
produce of their chase, she was always the first to run to
meet and welcome them.   She could not avoid admiring and
wishing for their simple ornaments, which appeared to her far
preferable to the brilliant decorations of the whites.

Shortly after Mary reached young womanhood a warrior, Sciakapa, informed her that her father was gravely ill
and wished to see her before he died.   Sciakapa guided her
through the wilderness and brought her back to Kaskaskia
after the death of Panisciowa.

After the death of her father, Mary related, Sciakapa
frequently returned to see her.   They soon became attached
to each other and in time he persuaded her to follow him into
the forest, where she became his wife according to Indian
custom.   Her action disappointed her white family, but when
they saw that she was happy, they pardoned her.   And each
year during the time the Indians were camped near Kaskaskia
she rarely passed a day without going to see them. [6]

While comparatively few Indian children were adopted
and raised by white people, a considerable number of them
were removed from their Indian families by missionaries or
Government officials and sent to boarding schools.   In their
eagerness to destroy the tribal structure and to make Chris-
tians and farmers of Indians who had lived by the chase,
these officials virtually kidnapped children on reservations and
sent them east to school. [7]

One of the Indian children who attended the white men's
schools was Thomas Wildcat Alford.   During his childhood he
had occasionally come in contact with white people and developed a "desire for things which civilization represented. "
He left the tribe at the age of twelve and attended boarding
schools for several years, seeking "a better way of living"
than his "people knew. "

Alford hoped that his experiences would be of value to
the Shawnees in learning to cope with a new way of life.   But
it was not to be.

"My homecoming was a bitter disappointment to me, "
he related.   "Noticing at once the change in my dress and
manner, in my speech and conduct, my people received me
coldly with suspicion.   Almost at once they suspected that I
had taken up the white man's religion, along with his habits

and manner of conduct.   There was no happy gathering of
family and friends, as I had so fondly dreamed there might
be.   Instead of being eager to learn the new ideas I had to
teach them, they gave me to understand very plainly that they
did not approve of me.   I had no real home to go to, and my
relatives did not welcome my presence. "[8]

An Indian who was strongly motivated during his boarding school days to accept white civilization was an Apache
named Jason Betzinez.   His life was one of amazing con-
trasts.   A young warrior in Geronimo's band, he shared that
ruthless raider's imprisonment in Florida.   Then he was
selected to attend a school for Indians at Carlisle, Pennsylvania.   After accepting white men's ways he became a steel
worker in Pittsburgh and fullback of the company's football
team.   Finally he returned to the Apaches and attempted to
lead them to the white man's road.   He married a white
woman and applied for land in Oklahoma when he could have
moved back to his Arizona homeland.   When Jason risked his
life trying to break up a medicine dance he was saddened to
see several of his former Carlisle classmates participating in
the festivities.   "Instead of showing the blanket Indians a
better way of life, the old Apaches showed them how things
had always been done, " he lamented.   "So the educated Indians joined the ignorant in order not to lose the good will
of the tribe. "[9]

Is there anything to be learned from this limited number of case studies as to whether the assimilation of Indian
children living with whites paralleled that of white children
captured by Indians?   The information given by Benjamin
Franklin that Indians invariably chose to return to their own
people carries great weight, and much evidence would be
needed to disprove it.   But it is evident from case studies
presented in this chapter that among some Indian children
living with white families the progress of assimilation closely
paralleled that of white children captured by Indians.   Patchy
Slaughter died at the age of four, but already she had attained many of the cultural traits of her adopted family.
Lydia Carter had been with the Chamberlain family only two
years when she fled into the woods to evade returning to the
Osage nation.   Mary, daughter of Panisciowa, eventually
married a warrior and returned to his way of life, but she
retained the Christian religion as well as close ties to the
white family which reared her.

A striking parallel to the correlation between age at

capture and degree of assimilation of white children is found
in the case of Maria and Bill Hockley. The boy was fourteen
when captured, his sister eleven. He retained his knowledge
of the Comanche language while she lost hers. The extent of
his assimilation closely approximated that of white boys captured at the same age. When the opportunity presented itself he rejoined the Indians. Not so with his younger sister.
Like eleven-year-old white captives, she quickly accepted the
way of life of her captors. How her story reminds one of
the attempts of redeemed white girls to escape from the
"captivity" of their original families! Much more evidence
is needed before reaching definite conclusions, but there is
some indication, at least, that the critical age for assimilation of Indian children did not differ greatly from that which
determined Indianization of white children.

In regard to the Indians who attended boarding schools,
it is evident that a considerable number of them were suffi-
ciently attracted to civilization to attempt to lead their own
people along the white man's road. Charles Eastman (a
Sioux), Thomas Wildcat Alford (a Shawnee), and Jason Betzinez (an Apache) were products of three of the most warlike
tribes in North American history. All of them were highly
critical of many aspects of white civilization, but they all
married white women and successfully adjusted to the new
way of life.

How, then, does one account for the large number of
Indian children who attended boarding schools and after years
of exposure to an advanced civilization rejected it to return
to the ways of their forefathers? The answer, perhaps, can
be found in the failure of the educated Indians to find a place
of esteem in either civilization. The demoralizing effect of
rejection of both races was described in a report by a com-
mittee which investigated conditions among Indians under
white subjection:

> An Indian youth has been taken from his friends
> and conducted to a new people, whose modes of
> thinking and living, whose pleasures and pursuits
> are totally dissimilar to those of his own nation.
> His new friends profess to love him, and a desire
> for his improvement in human and divine knowledge,
> and for his eternal salvation; but at the same time
> endeavour to make him sensible of his inferiority
> to themselves. To treat him as an equal would
> mortify their own pride, and degrade themselves in

the view of their neighbors.   He is put to school;
but his fellow students look upon him as a being of
an inferior species.   He acquires some knowledge,
and is taught some ornamental and perhaps useful
accomplishments, but the degrading memorials of
his inferiority, which are continually before his
eyes, remind him of the manners and habits of his
own country, where he was once free and equal to
his associates.   He sighs to return to his friends;
but there he meets with the most bitter mortifica-
tion.   He is neither a white man nor an Indian; as
he had no character with us, he has none with
them.   If he has strength of mind sufficient to re-
nounce all his acquirements, and resume the savage
life and manners, he may possibly be again received by his countrymen; but the greater probability is, that he will take refuge from their contempt
in the inebriating draught; and when this becomes
habitual, he will be guarded from no vice, and
secure from no crime. [10]

Swanton has pointed out that as a social being an individual treated as inferior by one group usually will allay
himself with another.   While it was possible for Indians living among whites (or for white captives held by Indians) to
conform culturally, it was impossible because of color differences to attain complete physical conformity.   This physical barrier to complete assimilation, Swanton believed, explained "those frequently cited instances in which an individual
of some race, Indian or other, has been taken from his
people, highly educated and, after an apparent conformity to
white ways, returns to his people and throws his civilized
acquirements entirely aside. "[11]

A study of Indian-white relationships reveals that the
original American was instinctively in tune with the world
about him and that an understanding of his cultural traits and
tribal life ways would have greatly benefitted the European
settler and his descendants.   It is indeed a pity that few
whites other than captive children learned what the Indians
knew of society "as organizer of man with universe. "[12] Had
this lesson been learned, perhaps the pure air and clear
streams of a once magnificent continent might yet remain for
our enjoyment, if not, indeed, for our very survival.   A
quarter century ago, John Collier wrote that "what the world
has lost, the world must have again, lest it die. "   And he
asserted that "the deep cause of our world agony is that we

have lost that passion for human personality and for the web
of life and the earth which the American Indians have tended
as a central, sacred fire since before the Stone Age.   Our
long hope is to renew that sacred fire in us all.   It is our
only long hope. "13

     While Collier, as Commissioner of Indian Affairs,
strove to restore the civilization of the demoralized red men,
the conquering race has moved ever more rapidly away from
harmony with nature and respect for the individual's right to
lead his life in his own way without intrusion.   Three gen-
erations of computers memorize and regurgitate incidents of
man's private life until individuality writhes in a coil of
whirring tapes.   And one once hostile Apache, Jason Betzinez, has lived to see the transformation of his native desert
from a last redoubt of the Stone Age into the incubator of the
Age of Nuclear Fission.   Captor with Geronimo of white
children, prisoner with his chief in white men's jails, convert to the white man's road, this incongruous Indian appeared on a national network at the age of ninety-six to pro-
test that television distorted the ancient Apache life way.
The quality of future American life will testify whether he
was the last surviving North American savage or the final
free man to have enjoyed the fruits of an unpolluted continent.

Notes

1.   Walter Noble Burns, Tombstone.   (New York, 1929),
      342-50.

2.   J. W. Wilbarger, Indian Depredations in Texas. (Aus-
      tin, 1889), 186-90.

3.   Ernest Wallace and E. Adamson Hoebel, The Co-
      manches, Lords of the South Plains.   (Norman, 1952),
      295.

4.   Wilbarger, Indian Depredations in Texas, 186-90.

5.   (Elias Cornelius), The Little Osage Captive, (N. p. ,
      n. d.), 14-94.

6.   Auguste Levasseur, Lafayette en Amérique, en 1824 et
      1825, II (Paris, 1829), 302-23.

7. Collier, The Indians of the Americas, 226.

8. Alford, Civilization, 111.

9. Jason Betzinez, I Fought With Geronimo. (Harrisburg, Pa., 1959), 177.

10. Jeremy Belknap and Jedediah Morse, Collections of the Massachusetts Historical Society, 1st Series, V, 29-30.

11. Swanton, "Notes on the Mental Assimilation of Nations," 501.

12. Collier, The Indian of the Americas, 27.

13. Ibid., 15-17.

BIBLIOGRAPHY

Alford, Thomas Wildcat. Civilization. Norman: University of Oklahoma Press, 1936.

Allen, Orlando. "Incidents in the Life of an Indian Captive." American Historical Record, I (1872), 409-10.

Babb, T. A. In the Bosom of the Comanches. 1912; rpt. Amarillo: Hargreaves, 1923.

Bakeless, John. Daniel Boone. New York: William Morrow, 1939.

Ball, Bonnie Sage. Red Trails and White. New York: Exposition Press, 1955.

Barbeau, Marius. "Indian Captivities." American Philosophical Society Proceedings, XCIV (1950), 522-48.

Bard, Archibald. "An Account of the Captivity of Richard Bard." A Selection of Some of the Most Interesting Narratives of Outrages Committed by the Indians, in Their Wars With the White People. Ed. Archibald Loudon. 2 vols. Carlisle: Press of A. Loudon, 1808-11.

Battey, Thomas C. The Life and Adventures of a Quaker Among the Indians. Boston: Lee and Shepard, 1875.

Belknap, Jeremy, and Jedediah Morse. "Report." Collections of the Massachusetts Historical Society, 1st Series, V, 29-30, as quoted in John R. Swanton. "Notes on the Assimilation of Races." Journal of the Washington Academy of Sciences, XVI (1926).

Betzinez, Jason. I Fought With Geronimo. Harrisburg: Stackpole Company, 1959.

Biocca, Ettore. Yanoama. New York: Dutton, 1970.

Buckalew, F. M. Buckalew, the Indian Captive. Mason, Tex.: Mason Herald, 1911.

Burns, Walter Noble. Tombstone. 1927; rpt. New York: Grosset & Dunlap, 1929.

Butler, Josiah. "Pioneer School Teaching at the Comanche-Kiowa Agency School, 1870-03." Chronicles of Oklahoma, VI (1928), 483-528.

Butterfield, Consul Willshire. History of the Girtys. 1890; rpt. Columbus: Long's College Book Co., 1950.

Caswell, Harriet S. Our Life Among the Iroquois Indians. Boston: Congregational Sunday-School and Publishing Society, (1892).

Coleman, Emma Lewis. New England Captives Carried to Canada Between 1677 and 1766. 2 vols. Portland, Me.: Southworth Press, 1925.

Collier, John. The Indians of the Americas. New York: W. W. Norton, 1947.

(Cornelius, Elias). The Little Osage Captive. 1821; rpt. n. p.: n. d.

Corwin, Hugh D. Comanche and Kiowa Captivities in Oklahoma and Texas. Lawton, Okla.: Hugh D. Corwin, 1959.

Davis, Mrs. Elvert M. "History of the Capture and Captivity of David Boyd From Cumberland County, Pennsylvania, 1756." Western Pennsylvania Historical Magazine, XIV (1931), 28-39.

DeHass, Willis. History of the Early Settlement and Indian Wars of Western Virginia. 1851; rpt. Parsons, W. Va.: McClain Printing Company, 1960.

DeShields, James T. Border Wars of Texas. Tioga, Tex.: Herald Company, 1912.

Draper Manuscripts (MSS in Wisconsin Historical Society Library, Madison, Wisc.) 11 C: 62, as quoted in John Bakeless, Daniel Boone. New York: William Morrow, 1939.

161

Drimmer, Frederick. Scalps and Tomahawks. New York: Coward-McCann, 1961.

Dunn, J. P., Jr. Massacres of the Mountains. 1886; rpt. New York: Archer House, n. d.

Eastman, Charles A. From the Deep Woods to Civilization. Boston: Little, Brown, 1916.

_____. Indian Boyhood. 1902; rpt. Boston: Little, Brown, 1937.

Emmitt, Robert. The Last War Trail. Norman: University of Oklahoma Press, (1954).

Evans, George Hill. Pigwacket, Part I: Old Indian Days in the Valley of the Saco. Conway: New Hampshire Historical Society, 1939.

Fenton, William N. American Indian and White Relations to 1830. Chapel Hill, University of North Carolina Press, 1957.

Finley, James B. Life Among the Indians. 1857; rpt. Cincinnati: Cranston & Curts, n. d.

Franklin, Benjamin. The Papers of Benjamin Franklin. 15 vols. to date. New Haven: Yale University Press, 1959- .

Garcilaso de la Vega. The Florida of the Inca. Trans. John and Jeannette Varner. Austin: University of Texas Press, 1951.

The Handbook of Texas. 2 vols. Austin: Texas State Historical Association, 1952.

Hanson, Elizabeth. "God's Mercy Surmounting Man's Cruelty." Tragedies of the Wilderness. Ed. Samuel G. Drake. 1841; rpt. Boston: Antiquarian Bookstore, 1846.

Hill, George W. "The Captivity of Christian Fast." The Indian Miscellany. Ed. W. W. Beach. Albany: J. Munsell, 1877.

Hodge, Frederick Webb. Handbook of American Indians North of Mexico. 2 vols. Washington: Government Printing Office, 1912.

Horn, (Sarah Ann). "A Narrative of the Captivity of Mrs. Horn, and Her Two Children, With Mrs. Harris, by the Camanche Indians. " 1839. Comanche Bondage. Ed. Carl Coke Rister. Glendale: Arthur H. Clark Company, 1955.

Hunter, J. Marvin. Horrors of Indian Captivity. Bandera, Tex.: Frontier Times, 1937.

Hunter, John D. Manners and Customs of Several Indian Tribes Located West of the Mississippi. 1823; rpt. Minneapolis: Ross & Haines, 1957.

Jemison, Mary. A Narrative of the Life of Mrs. Mary Jemison. 1824; rpt. New York: Random House, 1929.

Jewitt, John Rodgers. "The Headhunters of Nootka" (original title: A Narrative of the Adventures and Sufferings of John R. Jewitt). 1815. Scalps and Tomahawks. Ed. Frederick Drimmer. New York: Coward-McCann, 1961.

Jillson, William Rouse. Indian Captivities of the Early West. Louisville: Society of Colonial Wars in the Commonwealth of Kentucky, 1953.

Kelly, Fanny. Narrative of My Captivity Among the Sioux Indians. Hartford: Mutual Publishing Company, 1872.

Kinzie, Mrs. J. H. Wau-Bun. 1856; rpt. Chicago: Caxton Club, 1901.

Knowles, Nathaniel. "The Torture of Captives by the Indians of Eastern North America. " American Philosophical Society Proceedings, LXXXII (1940), 151-225.

Lee, Nelson. Three Years Among the Comanches. 1859; rpt. Norman: University of Oklahoma Press, 1957.

Lehmann, Herman. Nine Years Among the Indians. Ed. J. Marvin Hunter. Austin: Von Boeckmann-Jones Co. , 1927.

Leininger, Barbara, and Marie LeRoy. "Narrative. " Pennsylvania German Society Proceedings, XV (1906), 112-22.

Levasseur, Auguste. Lafayette en Amérique, en 1824 et 1825. 2 vols. Paris: Baudouin, 1829.

Lummis, Charles F. General Crook and the Apache Wars.
    Flagstaff, Ariz.: Northland Press, 1966.

M'Clung, John A. Sketches of Western Adventure. 1832;
    rpt. Covington, Ky.: R. H. Collins, 1872.

M'Cullough, John. "A Narrative of the Captivity of John
    M'Cullough." Selection of Some of the Most Interest-
    ing Narratives of Outrages Committed by the Indians,
    in Their Wars With the White People. Ed. Archibald
    Loudon. 2 vols. Carlisle: Press of A. Loudon,
    1808-11.

McKnight, Charles. Our Western Border. 1875; rpt. Phil-
    adelphia: J. C. McCurdy, 1879.

Marcy, Randolph B. Exploration of the Red River of Louis-
    iana in the Year 1852. 1853; rpt. Washington: B.
    Tucker, 1854.

Mayhall, Mildred P. The Indian Wars of Texas. Waco:
    Texian Press, 1965.

Methvin, J. J. Andele, or the Mexican-Indian Captive.
    1899; rpt. Anadarko, Okla: Plummer Printing Co.,
    1927.

Mooney, James. "Calendar History of the Kiowa Indians."
    Bureau of American Ethnology, Seventeenth Annual
    Report, Part 1. Washington: Government Printing
    Office, 1898.

Muhlenberg, Henry Melchior. "Regina, the German Cap-
    tive." Pennsylvania German Society Proceedings,
    XV (1906), 82-89.

Núñez Cabeza de Vaca, Álvar. The Journey of Álvar
    Núñez Cabeza de Vaca. 1905; rpt. Chicago: Rio
    Grande Press, 1964.

Parkman, Francis. The Conspiracy of Pontiac. 1851; rpt.
    New York: Macmillan, 1929.

Peck, George. Wyoming. New York: Harper, 1858.

Peckham, Howard H. Captured by Indians. New Bruns-
    wick: Rutgers University Press, 1954.

Porter, Kenneth W. "Indians and Negroes on the Texas Frontier." Journal of Negro History, XLI (1956), 285-310.

_____. "Relations Between Negroes and Indians." Journal of Negro History, XVII (1932), 321-25.

Radisson, Pierre Esprit. Voyages. Publications of the Prince Society, 16. Ed. Gideon D. Scull. 1885; rpt. New York: Peter Smith, 1943.

Rister, Carl Coke. Border Captives. Norman: University of Oklahoma Press, 1940.

_____. Comanche Bondage. Glendale: Arthur H. Clark Company, 1955.

Rowlandson, Mary. Narrative of Captivity of Mary Rowlandson. 1682; rpt. Boston: Houghton Mifflin, 1930.

Schultz, James Willard. My Life as an Indian. 1907; rpt. Boston: Houghton Mifflin, 1935.

Sipe, C. Hale. The Indian Wars of Pennsylvania. Harrisburg: Telegraph Press, 1931.

Slocum, Charles Elihu. History of Frances Slocum, the Captive. Defiance, Ohio: The Author, 1908.

Smith, Clinton L. The Boy Captives. (Bandera, Tex.: Frontier Times, 1927).

Smith, Dwight L. "Shawnee Captivity Ethnography." Ethnohistory, II (1955), 29-41.

Smith, James. An Account of the Remarkable Occurrences in the Life and Travels of Col. James Smith. 1799; rpt. Cincinnati: Robert C. Clarke, 1907.

(Smith, William). An Historical Account of the Expedition Against the Ohio Indians in the Year 1764. 1765; rpt. March of America Facsimile Series, 45. Ann Arbor: University Microfilms, (1966).

Spencer, Robert F., and Jesse D. Jennings. The Native Americans. New York: Harper & Row, 1965.

Spillane, Edward P. "An Iroquois Chief." United States Catholic Historical Society Historical Records and

<u>Studies</u>, VI, Pt. 1 (1911), 102-08.

Stratton, R. B. <u>Captivity of the Oatman Girls.</u> 1857; rpt. New York: Published for the author by Carlton & Porter, 1858.

Swanton, John R. "Notes on the Assimilation of Races." <u>Journal of the Washington Academy of Sciences</u>, XVI (1926), 493-502.

Tanner, John. <u>A Narrative of the Captivity and Adventures of John Tanner.</u> 1830; rpt. Minneapolis: Ross & Haines, 1956.

Tatum, Lawrie. <u>Our Red Brothers.</u> Philadelphia: J. C. Winston, 1899.

Vail, R. W. G. <u>The Voice of the Old Frontier.</u> Philadelphia: University of Pennsylvania Press, 1949.

Van Every, Dale. <u>Forth to the Wilderness.</u> New York: William Morrow, 1961.

Wallace, Ernest, and E. Adamson Hoebel. <u>The Comanches, Lords of the South Plains.</u> Norman: University of Oklahoma Press, 1952.

Washburn, Wilcomb E. <u>The Indian and the White Man.</u> New York: New York University Press, 1964.

Webb, Walter Prescott. <u>The Texas Rangers.</u> 1935; rpt. Austin, University of Texas Press, 1965.

Wellman, Paul I. <u>Death on Horseback.</u> Philadelphia: J. B. Lippincott, 1947.

Wharton, Clarence. <u>Satanta.</u> Dallas: B. Upshaw and Co., (1935).

Wilbarger, J. W. <u>Indian Depredations in Texas.</u> Austin: Hutchings Printing House, 1889.

Wilson, E. N. <u>The White Indian Boy</u>. Yonkers-on-Hudson: World Book Company, 1919.

Withers, Alexander Scott. <u>Chronicles of Border Warfare.</u> 1895; rpt. Parsons, W. Va.: McClain Printing Co., 1961.

INDEX

Abenaki Indians: 126, 129, 133, 144-145
Abenaki, Marguerite: 129
Adoption: 13-14, 18, 26-28, 35, 37, 40, 41, 42, 61-62,
    77, 79, 97, 101, 104, 110, 113, 116, 120, 123, 129,
    140, 152
Aes-nap, captive: 47
Aikens, Comanche captive: 89-91
Aitizzart (Indian town): 80
Albany, New York: 126. See also Orange, New Netherland
Alder, Jonathan, Shawnee captive: 117, 124
Alford, Thomas Wildcat, Shawnee: 13-14, 154-155, 156
Allegheny Indians: 30
Allegheny Mountains: 103
Allegheny River: 67
Alloquepy River: 72
American Association for the Advancement of Science: 15
American Revolution: 103, 116, 119, 128, 134, 139, 141,
    153
Anadarko, Oklahoma: 36
Andele. See Martinez, Andres
Andrews, Charles M.: 6
Apache Indians: 25, 37, 38, 40-41, 46, 108-109, 149-150,
    155, 156, 158. See also Chiricahua Indians, Lipan
    Indians, Mescalero Indians, Tonto Indians
Apache May. See Slaughter, Patchy
Arizona: 85, 149-150
Arkansas: 46
Armstrong, Col. John: 67-68, 128
Armstrong, Robert, Wyandot captive: 117, 120-121
Armstrong, Thomas, Seneca captive: 47, 119-120, 131
Assineboin Indians: 93
Asu-que-ti, captive: 47
Aw-i, captive: 47
Aytchart (Hachaath) Indians: 79

Babb, T. A., Comanche captive: 47, 109-110, 132
Barbeau, Marius: 6
Bard, Mrs. Richard, Delaware captive: 99
Beals, Dr. John C.: 82

167

Bears: 59, 71
Beaver Creek: 69
Bee, Hamilton P.: 150-152
Benjamin, Ezekiel, captive: 139
Benjamin, Nathan, captive: 139
Benjamin, William, captive: 139, 147
Bequancour River: 129
Between-the-Logs, Wyandot chief: 122
Betzinez, Jason, Apache warrior: 155, 156, 158
Big Wolf, Comanche chief: 89
Biocca, Ettore: 7
Bisbee, Arizona: 149
Black Beard, Comanche warrior: 115
Blackfish, Shawnee chief: 103-104
Blackfoot Indians: 11
Blue Leggings, Comanche: 36
Blue Licks, Kentucky: 104
Boone, Daniel: 103-104
Boonesborough, Kentucky: 104
Boston, Massachusetts: 20
Boston (ship): 79
Bouquet, Col. Henry: 2, 30, 33, 45, 72, 74, 102, 138
Bow and arrow, use of: 46, 75, 110, 143
Box, Ida, Kiowa captive: 100, 107
Box, Mrs. James, Kiowa captive: 100
Boyd, David, Delaware captive: 57-69, 97
Boyd, John, Delaware captive: 58-59
Boyd, Rhoda, Delaware captive: 4, 58, 117
Boyd, Sallie, Delaware captive: 58-59
Boyd, Thomas, captive: 47, 55, 117, 132
Boyeau, Mary, Sioux captive: 21-24, 132
Braddock, Gen. James: 31, 130
Bradley, Isaac, Abenaki captive: 48, 116, 144-145
Brainerd Indian School: 152
Branding: 37
Brayton, Matthew, captive: 47, 117, 131
Breckenridge, David, captive: 69-72
Brewster, Rev. James: 85
Brickell, John, captive: 117
British Army: 29, 31
Brown, Adam, captive: 47, 131
Buchannon Fort: 103
Buckelew, Frank, Lipan captive: 110
Buffalo: 37, 93, 130
Buffalo Gap, Texas: 124
Butler, Josiah: 35-36
Butterfield, Consul W.: 128

Cabeza de Vaca, Álvar Núñez de: 45
California: 51, 89, 140
Canada: 19-21, 45, 53, 92, 103, 115, 126, 127, 128, 132-133
Canafatauga Indians: 129
Carlisle Indian School: 155
Carlisle, Pennsylvania: 33-34, 64, 155
Carnoviste, Apache chief: 40
Carroll, H. Bailey: vii
Carter, Lydia, Osage child: 152-153, 155
Carter, Mrs. Lydia: 152
Carter, Mercy, captive: 47, 132
Catholics: 19-21, 133
Caughnawaga (Indian town): 123, 126, 130
Chamberlain, Catherine: 152
Chamberlain, Rev. William: 152, 155
Chandler, Joseph: 36
Cherokee Indians: 152
Chicago, Illinois: 146
Chihuahua, Mexico: 45, 101
China: 79
Chiricahua Indians: 37
Civil War: 92
Cocopah Indians: 88
Coleman, Emma Lewis: 20, 132
Collier, John, U. S. Commissioner of Indian Affairs: 157-158
Colorado River: 85
Comanche Indians: vii, 4, 6, 25, 35, 36-39, 40-42, 44, 45, 82-85, 89-91, 98, 101, 107, 109-110, 115-116, 124-125, 127, 139-140, 142, 150-152, 156
Comancheros: 84
Conover, George: 36
Coureurs de bois: 45
Crain, Wyandot chief: 122
Crawford, Col. William: 134
Crook, Gen. George: 109
Cumberland County, Pennsylvania: 138
Custaleta, Lipan chief: 110

Dakota Indians. See Sioux Indians
Day, Martha. See Diaz, Martina
De Shields, James T.: 140
De Soto Expedition: 52
Deerfield, Massachusetts: 19, 21, 129, 133
Delaware Indians: 17-19, 29-30, 57-65, 66, 72-74, 99, 116, 128-129, 134, 138-139, 152
Delemattano Indians. See Huron Indians
Deming, New Mexico: 109

Franklin, Benjamin: 9, 155
French, Abigail, captive: 47, 131
French and Indian War: 26, 30-31, 126
French Creek: 72
Frenchmen: 20-21, 22, 45-46, 53, 56-57, 67, 68, 69, 103,
  111-115, 126, 129, 130, 133
Friend, Temple, captive: 47, 117

Garcilaso de la Vega: 53
Gauntlet, running the: 60-61, 97, 129, 133
Genesee Flats: 28
German language: 30, 34-35, 40, 45, 108
Germans (as captives): 25, 30-35, 38-39, 40-42, 44-45, 70,
  108, 123-124
Geronimo, Apache chief: 37, 39, 46, 108-109, 155, 158
Gibson, Hugh, captive: 48, 117, 132
Gibson, Owen, captive: 70-72
Gill, Sagen: 126
Gill, Samuel, Abenaki captive: 47, 131
Gillespie County, Texas: 40, 108
Girty, George: 117, 128-129, 132
Girty, James: 116, 128, 132, 134
Girty, Simon: 47, 103, 116, 127-129, 132
Girty, Thomas: 128
Gonzales, Levando, captive: 47
Gosiute Indians: 94
Grantsville, Utah: 94, 96
Great Basin (culture area): 51
Great Lakes: 114
Great Plains: 2, 51
Greater Southwest (culture area): 51
Greenwood Collection of Narratives of Captivity: 6
Gregg family: 103
Gregg, Josiah: 101
Groton, New Hampshire: 126, 127
Grouard, Frank: 117
Gyles, John, Malisett captive: 48, 117

Haag, William G.: viii
Hacker, John: 133
Hacker's Creek: 133
Hankin, Mrs. W. E.: 149
Hanson, Elizabeth, captive: 53-57, 116
Harmar, Gen. Josiah: 145
Harris, Mary, captive: 131
Harris, Mrs., Comanche captive: 82-84
Haverhill, Massachusetts: 129
Hawkins, Elizabeth, Shawnee captive: 139, 147

Heap-o'-Bears, Kiowa warrior: 42-43
Hibbons family, captives: 107
Hirrihigua, Timucua chief: 52-53
Hoah-Wah, captive: 47, 117, 131
Hockley, Bill, Comanche child: 150-152, 156
Horn, John, Comanche captive: 84-85
Horn, Joseph, Comanche captive: 83-85
Horn, Mrs. Sarah Ann, Comanche captive: 82-85
Horseback, Comanche chief: 110
Hunter, J. Marvin: 40
Hunter, John, captive: 47, 75-78, 117, 131, 146
Hunting: 28, 111-112, 116, 130
Huron Indians: 70, 112, 113
Hurst, Hannah, captive: 131
Hurst, Hanno, captive: 47
Hutchinson, Thomas: 126-127

Idaho: 92
Illinois: 85, 94, 146, 153-154
Indian Territory: 36, 46, 110. See also Oklahoma
Iroquois Indians: 10-11, 19-21, 45-46, 59, 99, 119-120,
    121, 123, 153-154. See also Mingo Indians, Mohawk
    Indians, Seneca Indians

Jemison, Mary: Iroquois captive: 25-30, 45, 117, 132
Jenkiklamuhs (Indian town): 66
Jennings, Jesse D.: 51
Jesuits: 20
Jewitt, John, Nootka captive: 79-82
Jillson, Willard Rouse: 6

Kanawha River: 120
Kansa Indians: 77-78
Kansas: 92, 122
Kansas River: 78
Kaschkaschkung (Indian town): 69
Kaskaskia, Illinois: 153-154
Kellogg, Joanna, captive: 132
Kellogg, Rebecca, captive: 47, 131
Kelly, Fanny, Sioux captive: 21, 92-94
Kelly, Josiah: 92
Kentucky: 2, 46, 103-104, 120, 124, 127-128
Kickapoo Indians: 75-77
King, Thomas, Iroquois warrior: 99-100
Kiowa Dutch, Kiowa captive: 45, 47, 123-124
Kiowa Indians: 4, 25, 42-43, 45, 100, 107, 108, 123-124
Kittanny (Indian town): 65-68, 128
Knowles, Nathaniel: 101

173

Mak-suh, captive: 47
Malone, Rachel, captive: 47, 132
Malott, Catherine, Delaware captive: 128
Mamalty (Indian town): 69
Maqua Indians. See Mohawk Indians
Maquina, Nootka chief: 79-82
Marcy, Capt. Randolph B.: 125
Maria, Comanche child: 150-152
Marriages (to Indians): 3-4, 7, 11, 12, 14, 16, 18-19, 20-
    21, 23, 25, 29-30, 36, 43, 48, 76, 80-81, 98-99, 100,
    101, 120, 121, 122, 123, 124, 125, 126, 127, 128-129,
    139, 144, 145-146
Martin, Comanche captive: 89-91
Martinez, Andres, Kiowa captive: 42-43, 44
Mary, Iroquois woman: 153-154, 155
Massachusetts: 19-21, 125-126, 129, 133
Matagorda Bay, Texas: 123
Matamoros, Mexico: 82-83
Maumee River: 145
Mayhall, Mildred P.: 139
Meeker, M. C.: 101
Mescalero Indians: 42
Methvin, Rev. J. J.: 42
Metzger, Anna, Kiowa captive: 108
Metzger, Peter: 108
Mexicans: 25, 35-36, 41, 42-43, 44, 84, 101, 115-116
Mexico: 35, 45, 110, 149
Miami Indians: 17-19, 134, 145-146
Mill Creek, Virginia: 99
Mimbres River: 109
Mingo Indians: 3
Minnesota: 22
Mississippi: 152
Mississippi River: 18, 19, 46, 51, 97
Missouri: 75
Missouri River: 78
Mixed-bloods: 4, 39, 99, 102, 120, 121, 123, 125, 129,
    139, 140, 144
Mo-Keen, captive: 47
Mohave Indians: 87-88
Mohawk Indians: 20, 111-115, 141
Mohoning (Indian town): 72, 74
Monongahela River: 72
Montana: 11
Montreal, Canada: 20-21, 114, 129, 130, 133
Moore, James, captive: 47
Moore, Mrs. James, captive: 100
Moore, Jane, captive: 100

174

Rogers, Maj. Robert: 126
Rosalie, Abenaki captive: 126
Ross, L. S. (Sul): 125, 139, 140
Ross, Lizzie, Comanche captive: 140, 146
Rowlandson, Mary, captive: 98
Rush Springs, Oklahoma: 140

Sabinal River: 110
Sackum (Indian town): 68-69
Saenz, Bernardino, captive: 47, 131
Sage, Caty, Wyandot captive: 117, 122
Sage, Charles: 122
St. Clair, Gen. Arthur: 145
St. Francis (Indian town): 126
St. Lawrence River: 123
St. Peter's Lake: 113
St. Regis (Indian town): 126
Sale-beal, captive: 47
Salisbury, Massachusetts: 125-126
San Antonio, Texas: 39, 115, 127
San Bernardino Ranch: 150
San Carlos Reservation: 149
San Miguel, New Mexico: 85
Santa Fe, New Mexico: 101
Satanta, Kiowa chief: 45, 123
Sault Saint-Louis: 20
Scalping: 2, 27, 40, 43, 54, 58, 65, 67, 90, 96, 103, 129,
    134, 145
Schomingo (Indian town): 69
Schoolcraft, Leonard, captive: 132, 133-134
Schultz, James Willard: 11-12
Schuyler, John: 20-21
Schuyler, Peter: 20
Sciakapa, Iroquois warrior: 154
Searls, Elisha, captive: 47, 131
Seaver, James E.: 26
Seco River: 144
Seminole Indians: 46
Seneca Indians: 26-30, 119-120, 122, 128
Shawnee Indians: 2, 4, 5, 12-13, 26, 46, 98, 103-104, 120,
    124, 128, 134, 138, 139, 152, 154-155, 156
Sheninjee, Delaware warrior: 29-30
Shingas, Delaware chief: 99
Shippensburg, Pennsylvania: 64
Shoshone Indians: 94-96
Silver Horn, Sioux chief: 92
Simeons, John: 73
Sioux Indians: 12, 21-23, 92-94, 156

Six Nations. See Iroquois Indians
Slaughter, John: 149-150
Slaughter, Patchy, Apache child: 149-150, 155
Slavery: 32, 46, 52, 79, 82, 86, 102, 115
Slocum, Charles E.: 15-17
Slocum, Frances, Miami captive: 15-19, 131
Slocum, Joseph: 17, 19
Slover, John, Miami captive: 117, 131, 134-135
Smith, Clinton L., Comanche captive: 36-39, 44, 117, 132
Smith, Dwight L.: 5
Smith family of Mill Creek, Virginia: 99
Smith, James, captive: 47, 117, 129-130, 132
Smith, Jeff, captive: 36-39, 44, 47, 117, 131
Smith, William: 2
Smithwick, Noah: 107
Society of Friends: 15-16
South America, captives in: 7
Spaniards: 45, 51-53
Spanish language: 45, 53, 109
Spencer, Robert F.: 51
Spirit Lake: 22
Starvation: 87-88, 130, 140
Stewart, Comanche captive: 89-91
Stewart, weaver: 58-59
Stone (boy), captive: 131
Stratton, R. B.: 85
Strauch, "Grandma," Comanche captive: vii
Studebaker, Elizabeth, Delaware captive: 4, 117, 138-139, 146
Succohanos, Shawnee chief: 124
Sully, Gen. Alfred: 92
Susquehanna River: 66
Swanton, John R.: 1, 6, 16, 44, 157
Swift, Thad: vii

Tack-horse, Delaware chief: 18
Tahan, captive: 117, 131
Tanner, John, Ojibway captive: 117, 132, 143-144, 146, 147
Tarbell, John, Abenaki captive: 126, 127, 132
Tarbell, Sarah, Abenaki captive: 126
Tarbell, Zechariah, Abenaki captive: 126
Tashees (Indian town): 79-80
Tatooing: 87-88, 101
Tatum, Lawrie: 36, 115-116
Taylor, Zachary: 125
Texas: vii, 4, 36, 40, 42, 45, 82, 89, 98, 100, 107-109, 110, 115, 123, 124-125, 127, 141, 150
Texas Rangers: 37, 41, 43, 107, 125, 127, 140

Texas Revolution: 82
Thompson, Nootka captive: 79-82
Three Rivers, Canada: 111, 114
Timucua Indians: 51-53
Tomassa, Comanche captive: 35-36
Tonkaway Indians: 41
Tonto Indians: 85-87
Topsannah: 139-140
Torture: 1, 2, 5, 27-28, 40, 52, 67-68, 89-91, 100, 101,
    107, 113-114, 128, 135
Traders: 72, 82, 84-85, 101, 107
Treaty of Fort Pitt: 135
Tucson, Arizona: 85
Turner, John, Delaware captive: 128

Ultra-Mississippi (culture area): 51, 102
Union County, Pennsylvania: 122
United States Army: 41, 85, 123, 125, 149
Upquesta, chief: 80
Urie, Thomas: 64

Vail, R. W. G.: 6, 46
Valero, Helen, captive: 7
Vaudreuil, Marquis de: 20
Venenggo. See Fort Venenggo
Virginia: 2, 3, 98, 99, 103, 116, 122, 124, 135

Wabash River: 17
Waco Indians: 141
Waggoner, Peter, captive: 47, 117, 131
War of 1812: 145-146
Ward, James: 120
Ward, John, Shawnee captive: 117, 120
Washakie, Shoshone chief: 95-96
Washburn, Wilcomb E.: 9
Washington County, Pennsylvania: 139
Washington, D. C.: 152
Wayne, Gen. Anthony: 124, 145
Webb, Walter Prescott: vii, 6
Wells, William: 117, 145-146
West (culture area): 51, 102
West, Edmund, Jr., 133-134
Westmoreland County, Pennsylvania: 116, 122
Wheeling, (West) Virginia: 116, 135
White Chief, Iroquois captive: 121, 131
Wichita Indians: 25, 124
Wichita River: 43
Wiishto (Indian town): 29